RETURN

THE SECOND COMING OF JESUS CHRIST

Kenny Underwood

ISBN 978-1-63874-867-0 (paperback)
ISBN 978-1-68517-361-6 (hardcover)
ISBN 978-1-63874-868-7 (digital)

Christian Faith Publishing, Inc.
832 Park Avenue
Meadville, PA 16335
www.christianfaithpublishing.com

All scripture quotes are from the New International Version of the Bible.

New International Version (NIV)
Holy Bible, New International Version®, NIV® Copyright ©1973, 1978, 1984, 2011 by Biblica, Inc.®. All rights reserved worldwide.

Author photo courtesy of Mollie Underwood Morgan
Interior artwork courtesy of Matthew Underwood

Printed in the United States of America

CONTENTS

ACKNOWLEDGMENT

Thanks to my wife, Nancy, who is my most cherished friend. Thanks for your loving critiques during our mornings together in Wake, surrounded by beautiful bird conversations.

To my children, Zach, Matt, and Mollie. You have become my teachers and I am overwhelmed with the beauty I continue to find in your loving hearts.

To my Breakfast Brothers that continue to provide inspiration and reassurance. Our Friday mornings have been a beautiful oasis allowing us to briefly remove ourselves from the world and to find Christ in each other.

Most importantly, all glory to our Savior, Jesus Christ, who remains my all-in-all.

INTRODUCTION

Wake, Virginia
December 31, 2020

As I write these words the dawn of 2021 is at hand. The past year has been one for the record books, in part because of a world pandemic, domestic political chaos, and civil turmoil. A common theme echoed by the media and repeated by my friends is "good riddance to 2020," as though everything will be repaired with the new year.

But there is surely more at play on our planet. Theologians are poring through biblical prophecy as never before, and the top-selling book category in the United States is religion. Church leaders are facing new challenges, and their congregations strain under the limitations placed on them by government.

Can you detect it? Something is changing. Humanity seems restless and wanting. It is hard to find contentment, and our compassion for others is dulled as we strive to carry on and to take care of our own. Loneliness is spreading like a disease, and so much of the population feels an unquenchable emptiness.

It is not my intent to highlight the difficulties we face; the media does a much better job than I could ever do of terrorizing society. But perhaps it's time to recognize the quiet voice speaking to us and warning us of an approaching finale that must be acknowledged. Perhaps, now more than ever, it is time to search the Scriptures seeking to understand God's plan for His children.

For those of us who spend time in the Scriptures, contemplating the second coming of Jesus is stimulating. Many of us scrutinize books and commentaries that offer prophesy analysis and diverse interpretations. But what about our family and friends who, for whatever reason, don't enjoy the Bible and don't attend church? I've watched too many times as Christians attempting to witness for Christ bombard the non-churched with complex religious talk and scriptural references only to receive a glazed stare of bewilderment.

Return is my respectful attempt to portray a synopsis of Jesus's second coming to someone like me. Someone that is confused and even discouraged by trendy religious terms and shouting preachers that expect me to understand their pretentious message. It is my prayer that this book will be received by all readers in the loving spirit that it is written and that the Holy Spirit will, in His unique fashion, use it to bring its readers closer to Christ. I pray also that these words will stimulate, among believers and especially nonbelievers, a conversation about the second coming of Jesus.

Even so, to acquire knowledge of the return of Jesus, we must look to the Scriptures. Hence it requires the reader to consider the Bible and to read the Scriptures with an open and hopeful heart. I have done my best to provide the appropriate scriptures to support the message throughout the book.

Jesus is our hope and the only way in which we will find salvation. He tells us four times in the book of Revelation (Revelation 16:15, 22:7, 12, 20) that He is coming back for us. His anticipated return is an amazing story, a story that we must carry forward as commissioned by Jesus Himself.

May the Holy Spirit assist us as we seek to understand and prepare for the return of Jesus Christ.

CHAPTER 1

Contemplation

Behold, I am coming soon, bringing my recompense
with me, to repay everyone for what he has done.
—Revelation 22:12

There is a special day approaching, a day that will change everything. It will be an event so astonishing that it is inconceivable to every soul. Yet every soul that has ever existed will be involved and transformed. It will be a day for which all of mankind subconsciously and even unknowingly waits. It will be the day of Jesus's return.

For believers, His return will begin a transformation into glory that will certainly be beyond our current comprehension. Everything will be changed. I believe we'll encounter wonders beyond our imagination. We'll start with new bodies and experience true love at a level we never thought possible. Things vaguely described in the Bible will become real, and it will be as though we can finally breathe for the first time.

For others it will be far worse than any horror show. It will be the sudden realization of an existence without the presence of God. The apostle Paul warns us, *"They will be punished with everlasting destruction and shut out from the presence of the Lord and from the glory of his might" (2 Thessalonians 1:9).*

In "Inferno," the first part of Dante's fourteenth-century poem *Divine Comedy*, a chilling inscription encountered by those entering the gate leading to hell ends in "*Lasciate ogne speranza, voi ch'intrate,*" translated in English as "Abandon all hope, ye who enter here."[1] The poem describes Dante and his guide as they enter into hell while hearing the anguished screams of those without hope. These are the souls of people who, in life gave no consideration to the message of the gospel, the souls who were merely concerned with themselves.

It is unbelievable to me that so many of us go through our lives and never really give the return of Jesus any sincere consideration. Yes, many of us study the Bible and we discuss briefly the events described as they relate to His return, but too often we leave our groups and get back to the duties and responsibilities of our world, unchanged. Amazingly, we file our discussions in the area of our consciousness that is labeled as wonderful narratives or even interesting speculation.

Tragically, for those that are not students of the Bible, the subject of Jesus's return is not given any real examination. Some have heard that He will return but don't know what it involves or what it means to them personally. In fact many people question His existence and thus really can't make sense of an incident so unimaginable.

Others classify religious stuff as brainless chatter by religious people who are shallow and squander their time on inconsequential fantasy. According to the Pew Research Center, 65% of American adults describe themselves as Christians, which is down 12% over the past decade. The religiously unaffiliated share of the population consisting of people who describe their religious identity as atheist, agnostic, or "nothing in particular" now stands at 26%, up from 17% in 2009.[2] If the numbers are close, this means that of approx-

---

[1]   Dante Alighieri. 1320. *Divine Comedy.*

[2]   Pew Research Center. "In U.S., Decline of Christianity Continues at Rapid Pace." October 17, 2019. https://www.pewforum.org/2019/10/17/in-u-s-decline-of-christianity-continues-at-rapid-pace/

imately 330,000,000 Americans, 85,800,000 publicly reject Christ. Amazingly, this is in a country founded on Christian ideals.

Whatever your belief, if we take the time to search it out, the Bible offers us an impressive collection of insight into His planned return. For example, Jesus describes His return in *Matthew 24:30*, *"Then will appear the sign of the Son of Man in heaven. And then all the peoples of the earth will mourn when they see the Son of Man coming on the clouds of heaven, with power and great glory."* He offers us further insight in *Revelation 22:12*, *"Look, I am coming soon! My reward is with me, and I will give to each person according to what they have done."*

Although much is written in the Bible about Jesus's return, nowhere are we told when the event will take place. Scholars have speculated about when Jesus will return for centuries, but none have gotten it right. *"But about that day or hour no one knows, not even the angels in heaven, nor the Son, but only the Father. As it was in the days of Noah, so it will be at the coming of the Son of Man. For in the days before the flood, people were eating and drinking, marrying and giving in marriage, up to the day Noah entered the ark; and they knew nothing about what would happen until the flood came and took them all away. That is how it will be at the coming of the Son of Man"* *(Matthew 24:36–39).* As it was with the people from the time of Noah, many of us spend the majority of our time focusing primarily on our own needs and desires and ignoring God. It is a favorite tactic of the evil forces of this world to replace one consuming diversion with another even more consuming responsibility. All the while these interruptions are given priority over time we could spend with God. It is important that we be deliberate in our efforts to hear the voice of God so that we will be prepared to meet Christ upon His return.

In C. S. Lewis's book *Mere Christianity*, Lewis provides his thoughts on the gravity of Jesus's return.

> God will invade. But I wonder whether people who ask God to interfere openly and directly in our world quite realise what it will be like when He does. When that happens, it is the end of the

world. When the author walks on to the stage the play is over. God is going to invade, all right: but what is the good of saying you are on His side then, when you see the whole natural universe melting away like a dream and something else—something it never entered your head to conceive—comes crashing in; something so beautiful to some of us and so terrible to others that none of us will have any choice left? For this time it will be God without disguise, something so overwhelming that it will strike either irresistible love or irresistible horror into every creature. It will be too late then to choose your side. There is no use saying you choose to lie down when it has become impossible to stand up. That will not be the time for choosing; it will be the time when we discover which side we really have chosen, whether we realised it before or not. Now, today, this moment, is our chance to choose the right side. God is holding back to give us that chance. It will not last forever. We must take it or leave it.[3]

Lewis's characterization is frightening and should inspire us to turn to Jesus and ask for His mercy and forgiveness. He advises us to make our commitment "this moment" and not to defer selecting what side on which we want to be found.

Similarly, Isaiah warns us to *"Seek the Lord while he may be found; call on him while he is near" (Isaiah 55:6)*. We have the opportunity now, while our hearts are still beating to make a decision that will have eternal consequences. So often we are pressed to accept special pricing or opportunities in today's world that carry the warning

---

[3] C. S. Lewis. 1952. *Mere Christianity*. Geoffrey Bles—UK, Macmillan Publishers, HarperCollins Publishers.

"today only." Isaiah's warning is similar; the choice will not always be available.

Make no mistake, Christ is coming back to establish His kingdom. The book of Matthew records Jesus's words to His disciples confirming His return: *"For the Son of Man is going to come in his Father's glory with his angels, and then he will reward each person according to what they have done" (Matthew 16: 27).*

It seems to me that comparatively speaking, we hear much more in sermons about how to live a Christian life than about the astonishing story of the return of Jesus. Granted, it is hard for us to imagine an event so extreme and the Bible offers us only limited details. Surely this is part of His plan, and we see evidence in the Bible that God has restricted what we are to be told. For example, John is instructed not to reveal what he witnesses in *Revelation 10:4, "And when the seven thunders spoke, I was about to write; but I heard a voice from heaven say, 'Seal up what the seven thunders have said and do not write it down.'"* Daniel is also ordered not to make known part of the prophecies delivered to him concerning the end times: *"But you, Daniel, roll up and seal the words of the scroll until the time of the end" (Daniel 12:4).*

Nevertheless, God has offered us plenty to consider as we seek to understand the mystery surrounding Jesus's return. We can be assured that He has provided the perfect amount of evidence for us throughout the Bible. It is now up to us to display our faith as we prepare for Jesus to return and rescue the children of God.

Philip Doddridge was born in London in 1702. He was the youngest of twenty children, and when he was born he "showed so little sign of life" that he was laid aside as dead. However, one of the attendants, thinking she perceived some motion or breath, helped him to recover. He went on to become a pastor and wrote hundreds of hymns to accompany his sermons, although none were published during his lifetime. [4] His friend and biographer Job Orton issued them posthumously.

---

[4] http://www.hymntime.com/tch/bio/d/o/d/d/doddridge_p.htm.

Pastor Doddridge beautifully reflects on the return of Jesus in his hymn "'Behold, I Come,' the Savior Cries."

> "Behold, I come," the Savior cries,
> "With winged speed I come;
> My voice shall call your souls away
> To their eternal home.
> "Awake, ye sons of sloth, awake;
> Your vain amusements cease;
> And strive with your united powers,
> That ye be found in peace.
> "Happy the man, whose ready heart
> Obeys the sacred call;
> And shelters in My covenant grace
> His everlasting all."
> These eager eyes Thy signal wait;
> My dear Redeemer, come;
> I rove a weary pilgrim here,
> And long to be at home.[5]

I believe it is time for us to consider His return in a real sense. It is time to anticipate it knowing that He has prepared a place for us. It is a place so remarkable that our limited hearts and minds find it difficult to produce a preliminary picture.

We must look forward with enthusiasm to Jesus's return as our world is surely experiencing the birth pains described in *Matthew 24:7–8*, "*Nation will rise against nation, and kingdom against kingdom. There will be famines and earthquakes in various places. All these are the beginning of birth pains.*" It is against this backdrop that we find comfort in knowing that He is coming back for us. His return offers us hope, and with it brings our salvation from a decaying world.

---

[5] *Rev. Philip Doddridge, D. D. 1755. Hymns Founded on Various Texts in the Holy Scriptures.* Published posthumously by Job Orton. Shropshire, England: Joshua Eddowes & John Cotton.

John quotes Jesus in *Revelation 22:20, "Yes, I am coming soon."* And then John adds his own prayer, *"Amen. Come, Lord Jesus."* Let us also add our own prayer request to John's. *Amen. Come, Lord Jesus.*

CHAPTER 2

The Kingdom of God

*For our struggle is not against flesh and blood, but
against the rulers, against the authorities, against
the powers of this dark world and against the spiritual forces of evil in the heavenly realms.*
—*Ephesians 6:12*

The Bible gives us hints of an invisible world that operates continually and is just out of our perception. There is a fierce battle
raging between good and evil in a place or dimension that we do not
understand. For example, there are several accounts in the Bible of
angels and saints that have appeared to people on earth. So where do
they reside? Paul tells us in a cautious manner about the third heaven
that he was taken to during his vision on the road to Damascus. He
explained that he was *"was caught up to paradise and heard inexpressible things, things that no one is permitted to tell" (2 Corinthians 12:4).*

Jesus gives us insight into a world invisible to us when He tells
us about Lazarus and the rich man in Luke 16:19–31. He tells us that
when both men died, the angels carried Lazarus, a poor beggar, to
paradise. The rich man was sent to hell, a place of torment. The two

places are separated by a fixed chasm that could not be crossed. Jesus offers several precise details about both men and the conversation that took place, which included Abraham who was at Lazarus's side in paradise.

In another example, when Jesus was being arrested in the garden of Gethsemane He cautioned His companions not to resist. He referenced His kingdom when He said to them, *"Do you think I cannot call on my Father, and he will at once put at my disposal more than twelve legions of angels?" (Matthew 26:53).*

There are several other biblical examples offering us glimpses of a world that is somehow integrated with ours yet designed to avoid our perception. It appears to be a place where a lot of very important things are going on, and whether you believe it or not, you are involved and in the midst of a field of battle.

We find a great example in the book of Daniel describing events taking place in the heavenly realm. Daniel received a revelation from God concerning a great war. He prayed and fasted for understanding of the revelation, and God sent him an answer via an angel. Daniel's vision took place on a bank of the river Tigris. Imagine the following and place yourself in Daniel's shoes.

> *On the twenty-fourth day of the first month, as I was standing on the bank of the great river, the Tigris, I looked up and there before me was a man dressed in linen, with a belt of fine gold from Uphaz around his waist. His body was like topaz, his face like lightning, his eyes like flaming torches, his arms and legs like the gleam of burnished bronze, and his voice like the sound of a multitude. I, Daniel, was the only one who saw the vision; those who were with me did not see it, but such terror overwhelmed them that they fled and hid themselves. So I was left alone, gazing at this great vision; I had no strength left, my face turned deathly pale and I was helpless. Then I heard him speaking, and as I listened to*

him, I fell into a deep sleep, my face to the ground.
(Daniel 10:4–9)

Again, the vision was God's reply to Daniel concerning what God wanted him to know about a great war. He dispatched the man dressed in linen to explain things. The man in linen reported to Daniel the reason it took him three weeks to deliver God's message. *"Then he continued, 'Do not be afraid, Daniel. Since the first day that you set your mind to gain understanding and to humble yourself before your God, your words were heard, and I have come in response to them. But the prince of the Persian kingdom resisted me twenty-one days. Then Michael, one of the chief princes, came to help me, because I was detained there with the king of Persia. Now I have come to explain to you what will happen to your people in the future, for the vision concerns a time yet to come'"* (Daniel 10:12–14).

The events portray a profound glimpse into the angelic realm. God had dispatched an angel to answer Daniel's prayer for understanding. The angel had been delayed for twenty-one days due to an encounter with the prince of the Persian kingdom who was apparently a fallen angel. God's messenger finally gets help from Michael, one of God's chief princes.

It's telling that even God's messenger needs help in supporting us on earth. Michael, the archangel, was solicited to help overcome the prince of Persia. The word *archangel* means "angel of the highest rank." Most angels in the Bible are described as messengers, but the Bible reveals that Michael is described as a fighter or one who stands against evil spirits and principalities. Thus, he was sent to assist God's messenger so that the message could be delivered to Daniel.

I love to consider the heavenly realm and all that must be taking place around us as we walk along the paths laid out for us by our Father. The writer of Hebrews was aware that we are walking along a path created by the faithful that walked before us. *"Therefore, since we are surrounded by such a great cloud of witnesses, let us throw off everything that hinders and the sin that so easily entangles. And let us run with perseverance the race marked out for us"* (Hebrews 12:1).

Who is this great cloud of witnesses that apparently surrounds us? To me, the imagery seems to suggest that heavenly citizens are watching us and rooting us on from their celestial position. However, many people interpret the passage figuratively and explain that the witnesses are the list provided in Hebrews 11 and that we should take inspiration from them and act as though we are being watched. The writer of Hebrews references several of the saints that demonstrated strong faith on their walks. For example, in Hebrews 11:4, we are told that Abel offered a better sacrifice than Cain did. And because he did, *"he still speaks, even though he is dead"* to us. Surely these saints are included in the cloud of witnesses. Several other faithful saints are listed, and their lives should inspire us to *"run with perseverance the race marked out for us."*

Perhaps they are watching, or perhaps through their demonstration of faith, we are to reflect on them and their experiences as we run our race.

Personally, I believe an incomprehensible audience operates in heaven and that these heavenly hosts are aware of our existence and observe the happenings on earth. In Luke 2:8–13 we find the story of the angel that announced the birth of Jesus to the shepherds. After telling them about Jesus, suddenly a great company of the heavenly hosts appeared with the angel, praising God. *"Suddenly a great company of the heavenly host appeared with the angel, praising God and saying, 'Glory to God in the highest heaven, and on earth peace to those on whom his favor rests'" (Luke 2:13–14).*

In Revelation 19:1–5, John witnesses *"the roar of a great multitude in heaven shouting Hallelujah"* and praising God for the events *on earth* that have just taken place.

Paul tells us in 1 Timothy 5:21 that we are seen by God, Jesus, and the elect angels: *"I charge you, in the sight of God and Christ Jesus and the elect angels, to keep these instructions without partiality, and to do nothing out of favoritism."*

Albert Barnes describes the possibility that we are being observed by heaven's occupants as follows:

> It is not uncommon in the Scriptures to speak as if we were in the presence of holy angels, and of the disembodied spirits of the good; compare notes on Hebrews 12:1. No one can prove that the angels, and that the departed spirits of holy men, are not witnesses of what we do. At all events, it is right to urge on others the performance of duty as if the eye of a departed father, mother, or sister were fixed upon us, and as if we were encompassed by all the holy beings of heaven. Sin, too, should be avoided as if every eye in the universe were upon us. How many things do we do which we would not; how many feelings do we cherish which we would at once banish from our minds, if we felt that the heavens above us were as transparent as glass, and that all the holy beings around the throne were fixing an intense gaze upon us![6]

My dad passed away on June 28, 2019. He suffered for years with dementia, and his passing was in many ways a relief for the family as he had mentally left us months before his passing.

As his time neared, we began to notice how Dad would occasionally begin to stare across the room as though something had taken hold of his attention. He would sometimes smile and sometimes reach out as though he was attempting to communicate with someone unseen. There were times when he would even speak indistinctly as though attempting to converse with someone.

This is a common phenomenon experienced often by families in similar situations. Some in the medical community suggest that

---

[6] Albert Barnes. *Barnes' Notes on the Old and New Testaments*. Baker Books. 1 Timothy 5:21.

these loved ones are experiencing hallucinations brought on by pain medications. However, I'm not so sure. I have experienced this with other loved ones, and my intuition leads me to think there is more to these visions than pharmaceutically induced hallucinations. Perhaps our loved ones are encountering the unseen world that awaits us, the great cloud of witnesses? Perhaps friends and family that have previously passed are there to welcome them to their eternal home.

It's not just the heavenly occupants that are watching. Paul tells us in *Ephesians 6:12* that *"our struggle is not against flesh and blood, but against the rulers, against the authorities, against the powers of this dark world and against the spiritual forces of evil in the heavenly realms."* Here we have a hazy view of the fervent war that rages for our souls, and to me, it only makes sense that both the good and evil spiritual forces are aware of, and perhaps observing, the souls that they are so tenaciously pursuing or defending. This is the conflict that we must keep in mind as we walk along our life's path. We must be aware that we are caught in crossfire between good and evil and that it is real.

One might wonder how we can expect to emerge victorious when forces so mysterious and of such power, forces that we cannot even see, are at work. Our answer is that we must rely on the Holy Spirit that walks with us. Without Him, we are easy prey for the forces of evil.

Jesus promised us that when He left, God would provide a helper that will assist us as we navigate the world and wrestle with dark forces. Jesus said that the helper would teach us all things and remind us of the things that Jesus said. *"But the Advocate, the Holy Spirit, whom the Father will send in my name, will teach you all things and will remind you of everything I have said to you"* (John 14:26).

The Holy Spirit offers us the tools we need to withstand the attacks from dark forces that seek to pull us from God's grace. If we ask Him, He will walk with us daily and work within us to assist us in our decisions and actions. The archbishop of Canterbury, William Temple, provides us with a great example of how the Holy Spirit can gradually make us like Jesus and enable us to endure our journeys on earth. "It is no good giving me a play like *Hamlet* or *King Lear*, and telling me to write a play like that. Shakespeare could do it; I can't. And it is no good showing me a life like the life of Jesus and telling me to live a life like that. Jesus could do it; I can't. But if the genius of Shakespeare could come and live in me, then I could write plays like his. And if the Spirit of Jesus could come and live in me, then I could live a life like his."[7]

Friends, we are surrounded by a great cloud of witnesses. God's kingdom is rooting us on and doing things that help us along our path. Angels stand in the presence of God, and they battle for us as we make our way through this world. In addition to the heavenly beings, there are the saints that have gone before us. The author of Luke provides a list of a few of the saints that, through their faith, set an example for us to follow. The list includes Abel, Enoch, Noah, Abraham, Isaac, Jacob, Joseph, Moses, Rahab, Gideon, Barak, Samson, Jephthah, David, and Samuel. This is but a small fraction of the saints that eagerly await us, many who gave their lives so that we could receive the gospel. May we, someday, be counted among them.

There is within us a memory of a remarkable place, a deep recollection of a world without sin. It is a place where Adam and Eve enjoyed a pure and untarnished relationship with God. The human race has been searching for Eden, in most cases unknowingly, since the fall of mankind. Meanwhile, we are marooned on a broken planet. It is a place where evil *prowls around like a roaring lion looking for someone to devour" (1 Peter 5:8).*

We long for a return to Eden, for an untainted relationship with our Creator. We long for harmony with all of creation. It is a harmony that our inner being remembers but is impossible to fully comprehend in our current environment.

Friends, this will all change when the King of kings returns for His flock. The glory we are about to encounter will stagger the Most Holy among us, and we will begin a new existence.

Christ is coming back for us, and as Paul reminds us, every knee in heaven and on earth, and under the earth, will bow at His name.

---

[7] John R. W. Stott. 2010. *The Radical Disciple: Some Neglected Aspects of Our Calling.* InterVarsity Press, Downers Grove, IL. www.ivpress.com.

CHAPTER 3

The Fall

Then the Lord God said to the woman, "What is this you have done?" The woman said, "The serpent deceived me, and I ate."

—*Genesis 3:13*

We are not who we were created to be. God created the earth's foundation, including man, *"while the morning stars sang together and all the angels shouted for joy" (Job 7–8)*. Here the heavenly residents celebrated while God fashioned all that we know. At the beginning of creation, we were made morally innocent, but because of Adam and Eve's fall from grace, we are corrupted. Our hearts are now as described in *Jeremiah 17:9, "The heart is deceitful above all things and beyond cure. Who can understand it?"*

The Bible teaches that before the fall, Adam and Eve were *"both naked, and they felt no shame" (Genesis 2:25)*. This is evidence of their innocence. They didn't know what it meant to be clothed and felt no need to hide their true selves. Oh, how freeing this type of existence must be. Without care we would see the wonder and good in all things. Oh, what a day, when we can truly be who we were created to be and walk with our God and experience a kind of love that penetrates to the core of our soul. That day is coming again, friends. Paul encourages us in *1 Corinthians 13:12, "For now we see only a reflection as in a mirror; then we shall see face to face. Now I know in part; then I shall know fully, even as I am fully known."*

We are told in Genesis 1:27 that God created Adam and Eve in His own image. God's image is described in *1 John 1:5, "God is light; in him there is no darkness at all."* So Adam and Eve were in communion with God without darkness, living holy and enjoying an intimate bond with their Creator. God planted a garden for them, and God Himself walked in the garden. The beast of the field and all of the birds of the air were brought to Adam, and God watched as Adam assigned a name to each of them. Perhaps our souls at their deepest level somehow remember Eden and the perfect relationship shared there with our Creator. This explains why people talk about a hole in our hearts that nothing can fill. We work so hard to achieve success and to collect possessions that will fill the hole. These things may temporarily seem to satisfy us, but in a short time, they invariably fall short and we find ourselves once again seeking an answer to the emptiness within.

When Adam and Eve disobeyed God, the Holy Spirit within them withdrew and their fellowship with God was drastically changed. Consequently, all of mankind has inherited the broken relationship and continues to endure the unrelenting attack by Satan. We are told in the Old Testament that God, in His mercy, devised a way for mankind to have temporary exoneration and thus have fellowship with Him by sacrificing the blood of innocent animals. Later, God sent Christ to become the supreme sacrifice and thereby established a new covenant through His Son, a covenant that offers us salvation. *"For God so loved the world that he gave his one and only Son, that whoever believes in him shall not perish but have eternal life"* (John 3:16).

Because of the fall, we are flawed and sadly we are sinners. This is something that we must not take lightly. We must not joke about our sin and brush it off lackadaisically. Satan is devoted to our destruction and will use anything he can to lead us away from Christ. Paul warns us about Satan's deception in *2 Corinthians 11:3*, *"But I am afraid that just as Eve was deceived by the serpent's cunning, your minds may somehow be led astray from your sincere and pure devotion to Christ."*

In C. S. Lewis's book *The Screwtape Letters*, a satirical book addressing temptation, one of the devil's senior demons, Screwtape, is writing to his nephew Wormwood and explaining the process of leading humans down the path to hell. "It does not matter how small the sins are provided that their cumulative effect is to edge the man away from the Light and out into the Nothing. Murder is no better than cards if cards can do the trick. Indeed the safest road to Hell is the gradual one—the gentle slope, soft underfoot, without sudden turnings, without milestones, without signposts."[8]

Satan is constantly seeking ways to deceive us. He knows that we humans have our individual desires and weaknesses, and he targets those shortcomings. Paul tells us that Satan is the *"god of this age"* and that he *"has blinded the minds of unbelievers, so that they cannot see the light of the gospel that displays the glory of Christ"* (*2 Corinthians 4:4*).

I don't know how to even begin to think about what Satan must think of Christ's return. Surely he knows that the day is coming, and it must be his sole source of terror. Think about it, since he was thrown from heaven, his entire focus has been to capture as many souls as possible. Peter tells us that Satan *"prowls around like a roaring lion looking for someone to devour"* (*1 Peter 5:8*). Revelation also warns us that Satan is *"filled with fury, because he knows that his time is short"* (*Revelation 12:12*).

Among his many missions is to deceive mankind by persuading us to focus on anything but God. He uses whatever method he can to lure us away. His kingdom is here on earth, and his strategy comes at us in many ways and, more often than not, employs methods not regarded as classic sin. Distraction from God is one of his favorite efforts, and thus he encourages us to spend our time on unimportant tasks. He urges us to work long hours keeping us from our loved ones and overstimulates our minds with computers and televisions so that we can't hear the voice of God. He has launched hundreds

---

[8]   C. S. Lewis. May 2, 1941. "The Screwtape Letters." *The Guardian*.

of distorted religions over the ages convincing billions of people to worship the sun, animals, and imaginary gods. Satan infiltrates the Christian church and causes division and hatred between the denominations and even within individual churches. Too often our church leaders are so overloaded with good causes that they become deadened to the Holy Spirit.

The media is not immune to Satan's influence and continuously provides publicity and excessive status to celebrities and politicians that poke fun at the Christian community. Inexplicably, many people hold the opinions of musicians, actors, and political figures in high regard and listen intently as they share their opinions and beliefs. Unfortunately, a large percentage of the celebrity and political communities consider Christianity a farce and, even more disturbingly, consider Christians to be undereducated and shallow.

This quote from a celebrated comedian is a good example of how Satan employs perceived intellectuals to undermine Christianity:

> Religion has actually convinced people that there's an invisible man—living in the sky—who watches everything you do, every minute of every day. And the invisible man has a special list of ten things he does not want you to do. And if you do any of these ten things, he has a special place, full of fire and smoke and burning and torture and anguish, where he will send you to live and suffer and burn and choke and scream and cry forever and ever 'til the end of time! But He loves you... and HE NEEDS MONEY![9]

Trivializing Christianity is a true and tested method for those opposing Jesus. They attempt to use insecurity and doubt to influence people to join them as they play the role of the avant-garde personality. Predictably, there is no shortage of supporters falling in line with them and rooting them on.

---

[9] https://www.askatheists.com/atheist-quotes.

The devil knows that he will not go unpunished for his part in deceiving the world. We are told in the book of Revelation that he will be dealt with by God. *"Then I saw an angel coming down from heaven, having the key to the bottomless pit and a great chain in his hand. He laid hold of the dragon, that serpent of old, who is the Devil and Satan, and bound him for a thousand years; and he cast him into the bottomless pit, and shut him up, and set a seal on him, so that he should deceive the nations no more" (Revelation 20:1–3).*

The year 2020 has brought with it many challenges for Christians. We face what can be viewed as insurmountable obstacles. In addition to the pressures we face just to sustain our lives, we are daily confronted with increasing godlessness, terrorism, new diseases, and the constant political wars that we watch in real time. The list of Satan's tools is long, and Christians should expect to be his primary targets.

David Roper cleverly describes our adversary in his book *Seeing Through.* "Satan is a gentleman, Bacon told us. A charming fellow with immense power, subtlety, and thousands of years of experience. His chief aim, of course, is to injure the God against whom he once rebelled. To accomplish this, Satan misrepresents the Creator to his creatures, always attempting to frustrate his good purposes for them and hopefully—in the process—break the heart of God. Satan promises us the world, but as Milton said, 'All is false and hollow; though his tongue drops manna and makes the worse appear a better reason.'"[10]

Let's not fall victim to Satan's tricks. Focusing on the events happening around the world can confuse and frustrate us leaving us feeling helpless and demoralized. Too often we center our attention on the daily news as presented by various sources spun in a way to serve their respective interests. By focusing on these worldly struggles we allow immoral opinions to be placed in our hearts bringing about stress, discouragement, and even depression. While it is important to follow events, saturating ourselves with hateful and deceitful drama only pulls us farther away from our relationship with God. Christian,

---

[10] David Roper. 1995. *Seeing Through.* Sisters, Ore.: Questar, 22.

take heart, there is hope for those who believe. Just as Paul encouraged the Thessalonians, his words also speak to us from long ago when he tells us *"to wait for his Son from heaven, whom he raised from the dead—Jesus, who rescues us from the coming wrath"* (1 Thessalonians 1:7–10).

So how do we resist Satan's temptations? How do we attempt to achieve righteous lives in the midst of so much deception? Surely one of our main defenses is continually consulting the Word of God. *"How can a young person stay on the path of purity? By living according to your word"* (Psalm 119:9). Let's focus on the Scriptures and follow the examples offered to us throughout the Bible.

We must also accept the fact that we can never justify ourselves and become righteous by our good deeds. We must rely on the mercy of God and accept the grace that only He can provide. Our primary source of counsel and protection against Satan in this world is the truth of the gospel. The truth includes the fact that Christ went to the cross and that His blood covers us. His sacrifice makes us free from sin and offers us God's forgiveness. This is the truth of the gospel, and this truth, as Jesus said, *"will set you free"* (John 8:32). Free from sin, free from Satan.

It is true that the world in which we live is broken and sin is running rampant. The mistake made in the garden continues to make it difficult during our stay on earth. Nevertheless, we live alongside a world full of beautifully complex individuals searching, as we are, for hope and inspiration. And if we let Him, the Holy Spirit can employ us to reach those seeking fulfillment by sharing the wonderful message of Jesus.

We should take comfort in John's words as he was baptizing people in the Jordan and encountered Christ: *"Look, the Lamb of God, who takes away the sin of the world!"* (John 1:29).

He is coming back, my friend, and yes, He will remove sin and all things will become new!

CHAPTER 4

Loving the World

Do not love the world or anything in the world. If anyone loves the world, love for the Father is not in them. For everything in the world—the lust of the flesh, the lust of the eyes, and the pride of life—comes not from the Father but from the world. The world and its desires pass away, but whoever does the will of God lives forever.

—1 John 2:15–17

I remember a story I once heard about a king that had publicly encountered a wise beggar, and the king, feeling generous, offered to give the beggar anything he desired. The beggar smiled and asked, "Do you think you can fulfill my desire?" The king, offended, responded, "Of course I can, I am a king." The beggar produced what he called a begging bowl and asked the king to fill it with something. The king told his attendant to fill it with money, and he did. Immediately the king and the spectators noticed that no sooner did the money touch the bowl, it disappeared. Frustrated, the king had the attendant pour in pearls, diamonds, and emeralds; remarkably, everything disappeared into the magic bowl. The king continued with gold, the family silver, almost everything he had. Finally the king said, "I am humbled and ashamed that I cannot fill your bowl. I've given you almost everything I have. Please, before you leave, fill my mind that I should have one treasure left—the wisdom of knowing what it is your begging bowl is made of."

The beggar laughed and said simply, "It is no miracle and scarcely a secret. This begging bowl is made up of the one thing that has no limit. That stretches forever with no end. The bowl is made out of human desire."

Aren't there times when we all try and fill the bowl? We hope and pray to come across a better job, a bigger home, new cars, and even perhaps, a new life. We imagine that when some kind king comes along and drops these things into our bowl, then we'll be happy.

The Bible makes no secret of the price for letting the world influence our desires. *"You adulterous people, don't you know that friendship with the world means enmity against God? Therefore, anyone who chooses to be a friend of the world becomes an enemy of God"* (James 4:4).

It is true that most of the physical world around us is a beautiful place displaying amazing evidence of God. There is much to be appreciated and enjoyed if we just look around. However, the world around us is not as it was intended.

We are told in the book of Genesis that when Adam and Eve ate of the fruit, at that moment the world changed for all of us as sin entered the world. In Matthew Henry's commentary, sin is appropriately described as "the guilty cause of all the suffering that exists in the creation of God. It has brought on the woes of earth; it has kindled the flames of hell. As to man, not a tear has been shed, not a groan has been uttered, not a pang has been felt, in body or mind, that has not come from sin" (Section: Romans 8:18–25).

It is not only the heart of man that was corrupted because of Adam and Eve's disobedience. All of creation was changed, especially mankind's desires. Joseph Bension's commentary describes the universal change that took place with the *original sin*.

> Every thing seems perverted from its intended use: the inanimate creatures are pressed into man's rebellion; the luminaries of the heaven give him light by which to work wickedness; the fruits of the earth are sacrificed to his luxury, intemperance, and ostentation; its bowels are ransacked for metals, from which arms are forged, for public and private murder and revenge; or to gratify his avarice (greed), and excite him to fraud, oppression, and war. The animal tribes are subject to pain and death through man's sin, and their sufferings are exceedingly increased by his cruelty, who, instead of a kind master, is become their inhuman butcher and tyrant. So that every thing is in an unnatural state: the good creatures of God appear evil, through man's abuse of them; and even the enjoyment originally to be found in them is turned into vexation (irritation), bitterness, and disappointment, by his idolatrous love of them, and expectation from them. (Section: Romans 8:20–21)[11]

Our depravity has been brought on as a result of a gradual seduction by the evil one. We continue to find new avenues of immorality and indecency as we respond to a broken world that continues to deceive us by promising contentment and prosperity.

The third king of Israel, Solomon, is referred to as one of the wisest men to have ever lived. His accomplishments are impressive. He built the first temple on Mount Moriah in Jerusalem that became one of the wonders of the ancient world. He built amazing gardens, roads, and a fantastic palace. He accumulated thousands of horses

---

[11] Joseph Benson's Commentary. Carlton & Phillips; G. Lane & C. B. Tippett.

and chariots. He was an accomplished poet, writer, and scientist. Yet he could not find earthly contentment. In the book of Ecclesiastes, which he wrote, he talks about his search for happiness.

> *I undertook great projects: I built houses for myself and planted vineyards. I made gardens and parks and planted all kinds of fruit trees in them. I made reservoirs to water groves of flourishing trees. I bought male and female slaves and had other slaves who were born in my house. I also owned more herds and flocks than anyone in Jerusalem before me. I amassed silver and gold for myself, and the treasure of kings and provinces. I acquired male and female singers, and a harem as well—the delights of a man's heart. I became greater by far than anyone in Jerusalem before me. In all this my wisdom stayed with me. (Ecclesiastes 2:4–9)*

Solomon goes on to say, *"Yet when I surveyed all that my hands had done and what I had toiled to achieve, everything was meaningless, a chasing after the wind; nothing was gained under the sun" (Ecclesiastes 2:11).*

In the end Solomon offers his advice, *"Now all has been heard; here is the conclusion of the matter: Fear God and keep his commandments, for this is the duty of all mankind. For God will bring every deed into judgment, including every hidden thing, whether it is good or evil" (Ecclesiastes 12:13–14).*

Solomon's wisdom continues to speak directly to us today. He warns us that by focusing on worldly rewards we are destined to experience frustration and disappointment. C. S. Lewis sums it up this way: "Don't let your happiness depend on something you may lose."[12]

This especially includes money. Wealth cannot keep the bad times out of our lives. Actually, by making the accumulation of

---

[12] C. S. Lewis. 1971. *The Four Loves* (p.132). Houghton Mifflin Harcourt.

wealth our most important endeavor, we may even increase the number of lows that we experience in our lifetime.

It is not the money itself that can lead us to trouble; it is the priority in which we place on it. Fame and fortune, just like alcohol and drugs, can easily become the number one priority in one's life. It is easy to see this evidenced just by reading any newspaper or watching the news. Every day we hear of horrifying examples of people that have sunken to unimaginable predicaments.

So will a close relationship with God remove hardships from our lives? Absolutely not. Misfortunes occur in every life. Certainly most of us know people that we perceive to be good or godly that have experienced tragedies and/or public humiliation. Many people find it amusing to see a proclaimed Christian endure tragedy or, better yet, scandal. It has become fashionable to poke fun at many of today's more popular ministers and evangelist.

As a child of God we will not be spared the difficulties of life, but we will be given the strength to survive and even benefit from them. God repeatedly assures us of this throughout the Bible.

I remember a pastor providing an analogy using Michelangelo's masterpiece sculptor of David. Just as Michelangelo chipped away at a piece of marble, God chisels away as us. Michelangelo was removing everything in that chunk of marble that wasn't David. He worked long and hard, and if marble had feelings, the chiseling process would have been difficult and painful. But through the process, Michelangelo was able to produce the amazing depiction of King David that people continue to marvel at today. This is how God works with us. Through our ups and downs He shapes us, and although it can sometimes be unpleasant, we become seasoned and able to stand and represent Christ.

The key is to stay focused on our relationship with Jesus. To stay on track, we must continually pray and spend time in God's Word. It is also vital that we fellowship and study with other Christians. I remember a great African proverb that goes like this: "If you want to run fast, run alone. If you want to run far, run together."

When we move away or neglect our connection with God, we allow the world to insert itself into our lives. No one is immune to the seduction of the evil that roams the earth. Even Christian leaders that hold prominent positions within the church often fall prey. Some become focused on their positions and gaining recognition in the church. Some become obsessed with, as Sinclair B. Ferguson points out, the "intellectual fascination and challenge of the gospel and devote ourselves to understanding it, perhaps for its own sake, perhaps to communicate it to others. We measure our spiritual vitality in terms of how articulate we are, even how 'correct' our theology is."[13]

Of course we don't have a lot of options while living on planet Earth. We're here for a while and have no choice but to endure the war waged against God's children. Nevertheless, through constant communion with Christ and by exploring His Word, we can, as Paul tells us, *"Put on the full armor of God, so that you can take your stand against the devil's schemes" (Ephesians 6:11).*

If we can keep our eyes on Jesus and do our best to navigate around the *sin that so easily entangles*, our lives will have meaning and heaven will be ours.

In 1918 Helen H. Lemmel was given a brochure entitled *Focused.* The pamphlet contained these words: "So then, turn your eyes upon Him, look full into His face and you will find that the things of earth will acquire a strange new dimness."

The words had a profound effect on Helen, and she couldn't get the phrase out of her mind. She felt as though she was being prompted to translate the words into music as led by the spirit.

She explained, "Suddenly, as if commanded to stop and listen, I stood still, and singing in my soul and spirit was the chorus, with not one conscious moment of putting word to word to make rhyme, or note to note to make melody. The verses were written the same week, after the usual manner of composition, but none of the less dictated by the Holy Spirit."[14]

---

[13] Sinclair B. Ferguson. 2007. *In Christ Alone, Living the Gospel-Centered Life.* Reformation Trust Publishing.

[14] www.womenofchristianity.com, Women of Christianity.

Helen's song "Turn Your Eyes Upon Jesus" has touched millions of Christians and reminds us of the importance of keeping our eyes on Christ as we walk through a damaged world. And when we do, "the things of earth will grow strangely dim, in the light of His glory and grace."

Turn your eyes upon Jesus
Look full in His wonderful face
And the things of earth
Will grow strangely dim
In the light of His glory and grace.[15]

---

[15] Helen H. Lemmel. © 1922. "Turn Your Eyes Upon Jesus." Renewed 1950 by Singspiration Inc.

CHAPTER 5

The Light of the World

When Jesus spoke again to the people, he said, "I am the light of the world. Whoever follows me will never walk in darkness, but will have the light of life."

—John 8:12

In Genesis we find a magnificently understated description of creation. *"In the beginning God created the heavens and the earth. Now the earth was formless and empty, darkness was over the surface of the deep, and the Spirit of God was hovering over the waters. And God said, 'Let there be light,' and there was light" (Genesis 1:1–3).* Here we are a given brief glimpse of how creation began and how a dark and formless place was divinely lit, and by just four holy words spoken by God, light entered the world. Amazingly, we are told that God spoke creation into existence. Oh, how I look forward to knowing more about God and His nature.

Just as the universe needed God to command light, the world needed Jesus to bring light to a sinful civilization, and God sent Him. Isaiah foresees the coming of Jesus approximately 700 years before

His arrival: *"The people walking in darkness have seen a great light; on those living in the land of deep darkness a light has dawned" (Isaiah 9:2).*

When Jesus arrived in Israel the people of God were under the brutal control of Rome, and the Jewish religious leaders were ferociously competing for power. The Pharisees, Sadducees, Essenes, and groups of Zealots were often at odds and attempted to fashion their own respective versions of religion to gain influence.

Israel was made even darker due to the rule of King Herod, a brutal man who killed many of his subjects including some of his wives and two sons due to paranoia and ambition. Herod chose greed and power over the laws of God and opted to favor Rome over his own people. In an attempt to kill the baby Jesus, Herod ordered the deaths of all of the baby boys, two years old and under, in Bethlehem and its vicinity.

This is the darkness that existed at the time of Jesus's arrival. It was a cruel and uncertain world in which our Savior was placed.

Despite that, Isaiah goes on to explain the impact that Christ would have: *"For to us a child is born, to us a son is given, and the government will be on his shoulders. And he will be called Wonderful Counselor, Mighty God, Everlasting Father, Prince of Peace. Of the greatness of his government and peace there will be no end. He will reign on David's throne and over his kingdom, establishing and upholding it with justice and righteousness from that time on and forever. The zeal of the Lord Almighty will accomplish this" (Isaiah 9:6–7).* The new covenant impact began with the baby Jesus and continues eternally after His return and as He continues as our *Wonderful Counselor, Mighty God, Everlasting Father, and Prince of Peace.* As Isaiah tells us, this will all be accomplished by God's zeal. The Hebrew word for *zeal* used here is *qin'ah,* which infers an intense fervor, passion, and emotion. It is safe to assume that anything reflecting God's *qin'ah* will be carried out.

Jesus is still the light of the world, and His return remains a great mystery to us all. Yet in our meditation, when we search within our souls, we find a hunger which compels us to search deeper, more intensely for the ever so gentle voice that calls us to what we somehow know is our everlasting home. He reaches across the abyss through the Holy Spirit to engage us, to be an active part of our lives, experiencing every moment of our existence. And we can find comfort in the fact that Christ knows firsthand what we experience here on earth. He is well aware of the beauty and of the tragedy that we experience here. And His whisper to us, if we will listen, is that He will give us eternal life, and we will never perish; no one will snatch us out of His hand.

Knowing that He would soon be leaving, Christ amazed the crowds and His disciples when He spoke to them from a mountainside. Part of His Sermon on the Mount contains the following instruction: *"You are the light of the world. A town built on a hill cannot be hidden. Neither do people light a lamp and put it under a bowl. Instead they put it on its stand, and it gives light to everyone in the house. In the same way, let your light shine before others, that they may see your good deeds and glorify your Father in heaven" (Matthew 5:14–16).*

Jesus was preparing them, and His instruction continues to be relevant to us today. We are now the light of the world. We reflect His light into a dark world with the help of the Holy Spirit.

The concept of letting our light shine can be complicated. If we work too hard at displaying our work for the Lord, we are often viewed as self-righteous or prideful. Jesus warns us to be careful when we do good works and to *"not announce it with trumpets, as the hypocrites do in the synagogues and on the streets, to be honored by others. Truly I tell you, they have received their reward in full. But when you give to the needy, do not let your left hand know what your right hand is doing, so that your giving may be in secret. Then your Father, who sees what is done in secret, will reward you" (Matthew 6:2–4).*

Yet a number of scriptures instruct us to let His light shine through us so that others can see and know that our good works are done in the name of our Lord. Jesus tells us in the preceding chapter of Matthew to *"let your light shine before others, that they may see your good deeds and glorify your Father in heaven" (Matthew 5:16).*

Walking the line between a prideful and humble witness can be difficult, especially if we spend too much time and effort on our perceived behavior. Our walk with Christ is not meant to be a structured and obsessive balancing act. It should come naturally as the

Holy Spirit leads us. Through prayer and by study we achieve this righteousness divinely, and thus we are not required to manage a saintly posture on our own.

I ran across this quote by an unknown author which so clearly sums it up: "Don't shine so that others can see you. Shine so that, through you, others can see Him." When others see Him in us and realize that anything good we do comes from Christ, the balance we seek is demonstrated.

I am haunted by the memories of my grandmother and my dad's family. My dad was from Vidalia, Georgia, a really small farming town, and so as a boy I would spend time on my grandmother's farm. After my grandfather died she kept the farm and leased the land for crops. She continued to raise cattle and hogs. Nita Mae had spent her whole life on farms in Vidalia. She lived the humblest of lives, and when I think back, the picture I see in my mind of her seems to always include a Bible. When I was a young man my grandmother spoke to me very infrequently about God. However, God spoke to me through Nita Mae every time I was around her. Her personality, conversations, attitude, and just her overall being, showed me what it was like to live in the presence of God and to have a relationship with Jesus.

As I grew to become a man, I spoke more often with her about Christ. I was always amazed at the depth of her faith and her contentment. Her solid relationship with Jesus provided an example for me of how to live a life in step with Him.

Other women in the family were just like her. Aunt Gladys, Aunt Lucile, and Aunt Magdalene seemed to also walk consistently in the presence of God.

Not long before Aunt Magdalene died, I was blessed to be at a Thanksgiving dinner with her when she was asked to say grace. She sat in a wheelchair, her body twisted with arthritis. The most beautiful smile appeared on her face as she nodded yes. A frail but angelic voice began to permeate the air as Magdalene sang "Jesus Loves Me." I can't explain what happened while she sang. It was as though all of us were temporally transported to a different existence. We all sat in awe, as the Holy Spirit spoke to us through Magdalene. It was as though all of us in attendance were given a small glimpse of the peace and love that surely awaits all of those that follow Christ.

Nita Mae, Gladys, Lucile, and Magdalene are long gone, but their examples of how to live continue to speak to me today. You see, they didn't just tell me how to live a life of piety, they showed me. Even though they no longer walk among us, their lights continue to shine brightly today.

We all have within us the ability to accomplish some worthwhile endeavor. It can be like Nita Mae, by displaying a Christian attitude, or on the other hand it can be a very visible and direct mission or purpose. If we let Him, the Holy Spirit can accomplish wonderful things through us, many times, in fact more times than not, without us being aware.

After the resurrection Jesus appeared to the disciples at a mountain, where He had told them to meet Him. It was there that He gave them the Great Commission. The Commission was to go out and to spread the gospel. Essentially, Christ was instructing them to become vessels reflecting His light to the world. *"Then the eleven disciples went to Galilee, to the mountain where Jesus had told them to go. When they saw him, they worshiped him; but some doubted. Then Jesus came to them and said, 'All authority in heaven and on earth has been given to me. Therefore go and make disciples of all nations, baptizing them in the name of the Father and of the Son and of the Holy Spirit, and teaching them to obey everything I have commanded you. And surely I am with you always, to the very end of the age'" (Matthew 28:16–20).* These men, with the exception of Judas who hung himself, followed the instructions given to them by Jesus and, as a result, suffered greatly for their faith. It is a powerful testimony that all of them, except John, were reportedly martyred as they spread the story of Christ and the cross. John was exiled to Patmos where he wrote the book of Revelation, and some say he escaped after being cast into boiling oil. It is clear that their belief was without question and that they were so convinced of the truth of the gospel that they were willing to die. Beloved, this is also our commission. We are to reflect the light of Christ in every part of a dark planet.

I remember reading a story a minister told about a seminar he once attended in Greece. On the last day of the conference, the discussion leader walked over to the bright light of an open window and looked out. Then he asked if there were any questions. The minister laughingly asked him what was the meaning of life. Everyone in attendance laughed and stirred to leave. However, the leader held up his hand to ask for silence and then responded, "I will answer your question." He took his wallet out of his pocket and removed a small round mirror about the size of a quarter. Then he explained that when he was a small child during World War II, he was very poor. One day on the road, he found the broken pieces of a mirror. A German motorcycle had been wrecked at that place. He tried to find all the pieces and put them together but it was not possible, so he kept the largest piece. By scratching the largest piece on a stone, he made it round. He began to play with it as a toy and became fascinated by the fact that he could reflect light into dark places where the sun could never shine. He kept the little mirror, and as he grew up, he would take it out periodically and play with it.

As he became a man, he grew to understand that this was not just a child's game but also a metaphor of what he could do with his life. He came to understand that even though he was not the light or the source of the light, it would only shine into dark places if he reflected it. He said, "I am a fragment of a mirror whose whole design and shape I do not know. Nevertheless, with what I have, I can reflect light into the dark places of this world—into the dark places of human hearts—and change some things in some people. Perhaps others seeing it happen will do likewise. This is what I am about. This is the meaning of my life."[16]

Do we reflect the light of Christ into the darkness surrounding us? Will the world be a better place for our having been in it? God calls Christians to be active partners in spreading the gospel, to be the church. We have the opportunity to make our lives count and to share the most important story ever told. Each of us has a personal and nontransferable mission: to make Christ real in our own lives

---

[16] Robert Fulghum. 1991. *It Was On Fire When I Lay Down On It.* Ivy Books.

and to share His grace so that others may receive His salvation. Let's be the church where we are and help to resolve the crisis of spiritual leadership in our world.

Anyone that truly desires to can reflect His light. All we have to do is to open ourselves to the Holy Spirit and let Him speak through us. Take for example Ethel. After a Virginia supermarket was purchased by another grocery store chain, frequent patrons began inquiring if one of their favorite employees would continue to work at the supermarket. In fact, so many inquiries were made that the new management had a sign placed in the door that read, "Yes, Ethel is staying."

Ethel had become a favorite of many people frequenting the store because of her upbeat personality and positive outlook. When asked how she felt about what had happened, Ethel credited her religious beliefs for her warm disposition. "It's not me, it's the Christ that's in my life. When you've got the Holy Ghost, you just love everybody."

Ethel's life has substance. She was allowing God to display glimpses of His glory through her. Ethel's effect on the people she encountered is immeasurable.[17]

Christ is coming, and He will reward us for our obedience and for the good we do in His name. Jesus reminds us of His return in the last chapter of the last book in the Bible, *"Look, I am coming soon! My reward is with me, and I will give to each person according to what they have done" (Revelation 22:12).*

Friends, let's prepare for that day when Jesus, the Light of the World, will arrive to gather His people. We will receive our salvation, and the suffering of the world will cease. Children will no longer suffer poverty, abuse, hunger; millions of people will be released from the slavery and repression that they currently experience; the mentally and physically ill will be released from their affliction; addiction will be eliminated; our elderly will no longer struggle with pain and

---

[17] Neil Cornish. "Store won't shelve beloved clerk." *Daily Press The Times-Herald,* March 24, 1990, page 1.

loneliness. The world be healed, and we will have direct fellowship with Jesus.

In the meantime, we must be the hands and feet of Christ. We must continue to shine His light into the dark places of the world. Dwight L. Moody reminds us, "We are told to let our light shine, and if it does, we won't need to tell anybody it does. Lighthouses don't fire cannons to call attention to their shining—they just shine."

CHAPTER 6

Expectation

But about that day or hour no one knows, not even the angels in heaven, nor the Son, but only the Father. Be on guard! Be alert! You do not know when that time will come.

—Mark 13:32–33

Before Christ was crucified, He promised His disciples that He would return. *"My Father's house has many rooms; if that were not so, would I have told you that I am going there to prepare a place for you? And if I go and prepare a place for you, I will come back and take you to be with me that you also may be where I am" (John 14:2–3)*. Christ offered them, and us, this promise to bring hope and to help us while we cope with the corrupted world in which we live.

There are a plethora of references to the return of Christ in the Bible. Jesus referred to His return at least fifteen times in the New Testament. Of the 216 chapters in the New Testament, there are well over 300 references to the return of Christ. In the Old Testament, several of the prophets including Job, Moses, David, Isaiah, Jeremiah, and Daniel mention Jesus's return to earth.[18]

It is amazing to me that even Enoch, the great-grandfather of Noah, predicted the second coming of Christ. We find this in Jude 1:14–15, *"Enoch, the seventh from Adam, prophesied about them: 'See, the Lord is coming with thousands upon thousands of his holy ones to judge everyone, and to convict all of them of all the ungodly acts they have committed in their ungodliness, and of all the defiant words ungodly sinners have spoken against him.'"* This is uncanny evidence that God's plan for us was established long ago, long before He sent His Son to save us.

After His resurrection Jesus appeared to a diverse group of people including Mary Magdalene, who was at the tomb with Mary, the wife of Clopas. He appeared to the disciples more than once. He appeared to His brother James and what is estimated to be around five hundred people at the same time on a mountain in Galilee.

I love how the risen Jesus presented Himself on the road to Emmaus to two of the disciples that were walking the road from Jerusalem. One of the disciples was named Cleopas while the other is unidentified. While they were walking, discussing what had happened to Jesus, the Bible teaches that *"As they talked and discussed these things with each other, Jesus himself came up and walked along with them; but they were kept from recognizing him"* (Luke 24:15–16).

As He walked with them, Jesus let them describe what had happened at the crucifixion and about what they had been told of His resurrection. Jesus then told them, in *Luke 24:26–27*, about the need for the Messiah to *"suffer these things and then enter His glory."* He went on to explain to them, beginning with Moses and all the prophets *"what was said in all the Scriptures concerning Himself."* Imagine hearing Christ explaining all of the biblical references concerning Him. Imagine His demeanor and the assurance in His teaching. Imagine the grace and allure of His personality as He spoke to two of His beloved.

---

[18] "Does the Bible Teach That Jesus Will Return?" www.Christianity.com.

The disciples convinced Jesus to follow them and stay with them for the night. And as they dined, *"he took bread, gave thanks, broke it and began to give it to them. Then their eyes were opened and they recognized him, and he disappeared from their sight"* (Luke 24:30–31).

I can only describe the experience these disciples encountered as surreal. Perhaps they experienced something called piloerection, which is when humans go into a mild state of shock that causes the hairs on their arms and necks to stand up. Can you visualize the expressions on the faces of the disciples as they first looked at each other after Jesus disappeared?

The Bible then tells us in *Luke 24:32* that they asked each other, *"Were not our hearts burning within us while he talked with us on the road and opened the Scriptures to us?"* This is what an encounter with the risen Christ does. It just takes a moment, and we can be forever changed.

John Wesley, the great evangelist, described a similar burning experience, which took place on May 24, 1738. While he attended a meeting on Aldersgate Street in London, he recounted, "While he was describing the change which God works in the heart through faith in Christ, I felt my heart strangely warmed. I felt I did trust in Christ, Christ alone for salvation; and an assurance was given me that He had taken away my sins, even mine, and saved me from the law of sin and death."[19] Of course Wesley went on to help in forming the Methodist movement. Through the Methodist Church and teachings, God continues to bring about the salvation of many as a result of the efforts of John Wesley.

Have you experienced this "warming or burning of the heart" before? To me, this is a gift from the Holy Spirit. There are times when a verse of Scripture or an interaction with another person as we pray or discuss Jesus, when my heart will burn within, providing me with assurance of the presence of the Holy Spirit. These moments leave me changed and yearning for more.

Jesus continued to appear to people after His resurrection throughout a forty-day period. He spoke to those He chose about

---

[19] John Wesley. "Heart Strangely Warmed." http://www.christianity.com/

the kingdom of God. After His time was done, the Bible tells us that He was taken up before their very eyes. Those that were present looked intently up into the sky as He was going, and suddenly two men dressed in white stood beside them. The men asked, *"Men of Galilee, why do you stand here looking into the sky? This same Jesus, who has been taken from you into heaven, will come back in the same way you have seen Him go into heaven" (Acts 1:11).*

It is important to me to make a distinction between the events referred to as rapture and the second coming of Jesus. In the next chapter we will examine the rapture, which is when Jesus comes for His church. All believers who are alive, along with the resurrected believers (those who are dead), will be *"caught up together with them in the clouds, to meet the Lord in the air" (1 Thessalonians 4:17).*

Simply put, the second coming of Jesus is the term used to describe the incident when Jesus will return to the earth to conquer His enemies and reign as king. Many believe that His second coming will happen at the end of the seven-year tribulation period, beginning when Jesus returns to the earth with His feet landing on the Mount of Olives east of Jerusalem.

Both of these events will transform everything that we know.

As I mentioned previously, there are several interpretations of how the final days will take place. A popular belief is that the events will take place in this order:

1. Rapture—Christ will return, *in the air*, for His church, and all believers both dead and alive will be taken to be with Him. This will begin the seven-year tribulation period.
2. Jesus's second coming—To end the tribulation, Jesus will return to the earth and set up His one-thousand-year millennial kingdom. Satan will be bound throughout the thousand years.
3. Final judgment—Christ will convene court, and every soul will stand before Him in final judgment. Books will be opened, and every person to have ever lived will be judged. Although some believe that Christians and nonbelievers will be judged separately, all will stand before Jesus for judg-

ment. Unbelievers will be sentenced to hell, and believers will finally come to understand the breadth of grace provided to them by Jesus as they join Him for eternity.

Once again, let us not get caught up debating how or when these events will take place. The truth is that nobody on this side of heaven knows for sure. Our perceived understanding will not change anything. Christ is coming, and only the Father knows how and when. I wholeheartedly suggest you spend time in the Scriptures and decipher for yourself, through prayer and study, what the Scriptures say about the events leading up to Jesus's return.

All of mankind should earnestly consider the information presented throughout the Bible concerning the return of Jesus. Mark warns us, *"Therefore keep watch because you do not know when the owner of the house will come back—whether in the evening, or at midnight, or when the rooster crows, or at dawn. If he comes suddenly, do not let him find you sleeping. What I say to you, I say to everyone: 'Watch!'"* *(Mark 13:35–37)*. Mark is telling us to observe, to look around us, and to make sure we're found doing our best to follow His teachings.

The Scriptures offers us insight into several phenomena that will take place before the return of Christ.

Christians will abandon the faith

Paul tells us in 1 Timothy 4:1 about a *falling away* from belief in God: *"The Spirit clearly says that in later times some will abandon the faith and follow deceiving spirits and things taught by demons."*

It's no secret that Christian church attendance across the world continues to decline. In addition, God's Word is increasingly being polluted by a variety of fashionable worship styles that change the meaning of the Scriptures to conform to the desires of man. New-age teachers publish and broadcast biblical interpretations that find favor with those not willing to accept the truth as presented in the Scriptures. Paul warns us, *"For the time will come when people will not put up with sound doctrine. Instead, to suit their own desires, they will gather around them a great number of teachers to say what their itching ears want to hear. They will turn their ears away from the truth and turn aside to myths."*

Love of many will grow cold

One of Jesus's answers when asked "What will be the sign of your coming?" was *"Because of the increase of wickedness, the love of most will grow cold, but the one who stands firm to the end will be saved" (Matthew 24:12–13).* I find this statement to be especially troubling in the NIV translation above. Jesus says the love of *most* will grow cold. Other translations use the word *many.* Both indicate that a large portion of mankind will lose what binds us together as human beings: love.

Paul also warns us that people will lose their love for one another and focus selfishly on themselves. *"But mark this: There will be terrible times in the last days. People will be lovers of themselves, lovers of money, boastful, proud, abusive, disobedient to their parents, ungrateful, unholy, without love, unforgiving, slanderous, without self-control, brutal, not lovers of the good, treacherous, rash, conceited, lovers of pleasure rather than lovers of God" (2 Timothy 3:1–4).* These patterns of behavior are easy to see in today's daily news reports. Unfortunately, if we look closely, we all too often recognize this trend in our family and friends. Many of us are so caught up in the struggle for perceived worldly success that we can't hear the voice of God. We must be deliberate in our efforts to spend time with Him. If not, our hearts will harden and we will become jaded and vulnerable to worldly influences.

Persecution

Jesus Himself warns us of the persecution to come before the end of the age as recorded in Luke 21:12, *"But before all this, they will seize you and persecute you. They will hand you over to synagogues and put you in prison, and you will be brought before kings and governors, and all on account of my name.*"

The organization OpenDoors[20] reports in their 2020 World Watch List that *in the last year:*

- over 260 million Christians are living in places where they experience high levels of persecution;
- 2,983 Christians have been killed for their faith;
- 9,488 churches and other Christian buildings have been attacked; and
- large numbers of believers have been detained without trial.

Those who are physically persecuted are only a small fraction of God's children that are victimized throughout the world today. Increasingly it has become fashionable to poke fun at Christianity as being for the uneducated or unsophisticated. Perceived intellectuals that project a false enlightenment dismiss the opinions of the faithful smugly as though their opinions are shallow and fictitious. Increasingly, Christians are pressed to keep quiet or to face assault from the world. This is the opposite of what Christ instructs us to do: *"He said to them, 'Go into all the world and preach the gospel to all creation'" (Mark 16:15).*

We must remain bold in our witness for Jesus, standing strong against the tide of persecution that rushes at us daily.

Wars and rumors of wars

Jesus gives us insight in Matthew 24 about something He calls "*the beginning of birth pains,*" which will become evident just before His return. "*You will hear of wars and rumors of wars, but see to it that you are not alarmed. Such things must happen, but the end is still to come. Nation will rise against nation, and kingdom against kingdom.*

---

[20] Opendoorsusa.org

There will be famines and earthquakes in various places. All these are the beginning of birth pains" (Matthew 24:6–8).

Christians as well as non-Christians universally quote these familiar words given to us by Jesus. Sadly, wars and rumor of wars are one of the more apparent of Jesus's list to recognize. Conflicts between countries are nothing new; however, the modern-day battlefield has changed. The list of weapons has expanded and now includes cyber and biological technologies and an additional inventory of horrific weaponry that can easily destroy millions.

Gospel preached worldwide

In Matthew 24:14 Jesus makes an interesting comment about the gospel being preached to the whole world, *"And this gospel of the kingdom will be preached in the whole world as a testimony to all nations, and then the end will come."* Never before has the world been so connected as it is today. According to Internet World Stats, there were over 4.5 billion Internet users as of March 2020.[21] Therefore, a large percentage of these users have access to the gospel. Include television, newspapers, books, and an abundance of global ministries and it becomes clear that the world today enjoys access to the gospel as never before in the history of mankind. It is uncommon to find a society today that has not been exposed to the gospel of Jesus Christ. To me, this is one of the more noteworthy developments to be considered as we anticipate Christ's return.

Israel restored

Perhaps one of the most important events to take place before Jesus returns has already happened. In 1948 Israel was recognized as a sovereign state for the first time since AD 70. Many prophecies refer to the importance of Israel being restored. The Bible tells us that

---

[21] Internetworldstats.com

the Jewish people would return to Israel and that Jerusalem will be at the center of end-time events.

Luke 21:20 advises us to watch Jerusalem closely, *"When you see Jerusalem being surrounded by armies, you will know that its desolation is near."* Clearly, the situation today in Israel fits this description.

- In Lebanon, on the northern border, Hezbollah maintains hundreds of thousands of missiles pointed at Israeli cities.
- Iran is flooding Syria with Iranian soldiers building an army targeted at Israel's destruction.
- Russia is building large Air Force and military bases on the Syrian coast.
- Hamas is stockpiling missiles and building tunnels into Israel's southern border in preparation for an attack.
- The Palestinian authority is in the midst of establishing Intifada all over Israel.

Jerusalem will unquestionably be the city where most of the significant events will take place as we await the return of Jesus. Thus we should carefully scrutinize current events there as they play out.

Jerusalem's history is like no other place on earth. Consider the following:

- It was captured by King David over 3,000 years ago and established as the national capital of Israel.
- David's son Solomon erected the Temple of Solomon, which became the center of worship for the Hebrews.
- It is the place where the Messiah Jesus was betrayed at Gethsemane.
- It is the place where the pardoning of Barabbas took place.
- It is where Jesus carried the cross, along the Via Dolorosa, to Golgotha.
- It is the place where Christ was crucified.
- It is the place of Jesus's resurrection.
- It is the place where the Bible tells us Jesus will return for the second coming.

- Judaism, Islam, and Christianity consider it holy and continue to struggle for control.

These are but a few of the noteworthy truths concerning Jerusalem. The list is long, but these facts are only a prelude to the astounding events that will occur in the future. These events will cause the whole world to tremble. *"People will flee to caves in the rocks and to holes in the ground from the fearful presence of the Lord and the splendor of his majesty, when he rises to shake the earth" (Isaiah 2:19).*

I find Charles Spurgeon's comments about the second coming of Jesus to be profound. He points out that if we remain vigilant and expectant of Jesus's return, we will be prepared when Christ comes.

His desire is that we may have confidence if he appear on a sudden. What does he mean by having confidence when he shall appear? Why, this: that if you abide in him when you do not see him, you will be very bold should he suddenly reveal himself. Before he appears, you have dwelt in him, and he has dwelt in you; what fear could his appearing cause you? Faith has so realized him, that if suddenly he were to appear to the senses, it would be no surprise to you; and, assuredly, it would cause you joy rather than dismay. You would feel that you at last enjoyed what you had long expected, and saw somewhat more closely a friend with whom you had long been familiar. I trust, beloved, that some of us live in such a style that if, on a sudden, our Lord were to appear, it would cause no alarm to us. We have believed him to be present, though unseen, and it will not affect our conduct when he steps from behind the curtain, and stands in the open light. O Lord Jesus, if thou wert now to stand in our midst, we should remember that we had thy presence before, and lived in it, and now we should only be the more assured of that which we before knew by faith. We shall behold our Lord with confidence, freedom, assurance, and delight, feeling perfectly at home with him. The believer who abides in his Lord would be but little startled by his sudden appearing; he is serving his Lord now, and he would go on serving him; he loves him now, and he would go on loving him, only as he would have a clearer view of him, he would feel a more intense consecration to him.[22]

Spurgeon's comments reveal a deep-seated faith and trust in his relationship with Jesus. It is beyond a superficial pretense or showiness. Don't get me wrong; faith displayed in any manner is useful to Jesus. Nevertheless, Spurgeon is displaying a level of confidence that we should attempt to achieve, knowing that the promises of Christ are real and that it's only a matter of time before they are realized.

Mankind is continually attempting to use the Scriptures to predict the precise time of Jesus's return. Clearly, if God wanted us to know exactly when His Son would come back, we would know. I believe God's purpose in providing us with prophecies relating to Christ's return is to keep us looking to Him for answers. He wants our relationships to be dynamic and interactive and for us to demonstrate our faith in His promises. Moses tells us in *Deuteronomy 29:29, "The secret things belong to the Lord our God, but the things revealed belong to us and to our children forever, that we may follow all the words of this law."*

Let's be watchful but composed as we await the return of our Savior. He knows our hearts and is aware of our questions and insecurities. He will not disappoint. He loves us and knows us individually better than we know ourselves. Stay strong in your faith, my friends. It will be just a moment before all will be revealed.

---

[22] Charles Haddon Spurgeon. September 22, 1889. Scripture: 1 John 2:28 From: Metropolitan Tabernacle Pulpit Volume 35.

CHAPTER 7

Rapture

For the Lord himself will come down from heaven, with a loud command, with the voice of the archangel and with the trumpet call of God, and the dead in Christ will rise first. After that, we who are still alive and are left will be caught up together with them in the clouds to meet the Lord in the air. And so we will be with the Lord forever.
—*1 Thessalonians 4:16–17*

The study and research into end times, or eschatology, has become the focus of so many in the church today. The varied interpretations presented in a large array of books, videos, and sermons can even confuse the most dedicated scholars. It is easy to get caught up in the details and miss the principal point, that Jesus will be returning and will gather His church to be with Him.

In the Bible we find several prophetic scriptures that reference an awe-inspiring event that is clearly yet another fascinating mystery for mankind to ponder. The event described in 1 Thessalonians 4 is generally referred to as the rapture. The word *rapture* is derived from the Latin verb *rapere*, translated as "carry off" or to "catch up." The term "rapture" is not found in the Bible, and much controversy surrounds the issue. My intent here is not to support or deny any specific interpretation of the rapture as described by theologians and scholars; however, the fact that the scriptures are unquestionably describing Jesus returning for His children is undeniable. Call it what you will, the Bible is offering us a preview of Christ coming for His church. As is always the case with man, we attempt to explain the chronology and the described events in our own terms. Let's examine the event as it is described in the Bible.

We are told in the book of Luke that Christ's return will surprise mankind and that, just like in the days of Noah, *"People will be eating, drinking, marrying and being given in marriage up to the day Noah entered the ark. Then the flood came and destroyed them all" (Luke 17:27).* The Bible explains that it will be similar to this on the day the Son of Man is revealed. *"On that day no one who is on the housetop, with possessions inside, should go down to get them. Likewise, no one in the field should go back for anything. Remember Lot's wife! Whoever tries to keep their life will lose it, and whoever loses their life will preserve it. I tell you, on that night two people will be in one bed; one will be taken and the other left. Two women will be grinding grain together; one will be taken and the other left" (Luke 17:31–36).*

It is clear that this is not a gradual occurrence. Paul tells us in 1 Corinthians that it will happen very suddenly. *"Listen, I tell you a mystery: We will not all sleep, but we will all be changed—in a flash, in the twinkling of an eye, at the last trumpet. For the trumpet will sound, the dead will be raised imperishable, and we will be changed" (1 Corinthians 15:51–52).* How fast is the twinkling of an eye? This description is particularly profound to me because it indicates how surprised we will all be. In one moment we may be conducting a meeting, tilling a garden, feeding a baby. In the next, we will be in the magnificent presence of Christ.

As I mentioned before, scholars differ on the timing and sequence of the rapture. Some do not recognize the rapture at all and contend that Christ's return will be at His second coming when He will establish His kingdom on earth. I encourage you to spend time in the Scriptures and to decide for yourself your view of how the return of Jesus will be played out. The point is, that at some moment in time, Christ will come quickly and without warning. Thus, we as Christians should be vigilant and live our lives in preparation for His return.

Years ago, I was troubled how a coworker responded when I asked him when he and his family would start going to church. He had been giving me the idea that he was a believer but really didn't want to talk about Christ. He nonchalantly explained to me that they would start when things slowed down and he could find time. It's been over twenty-five years, and I don't think "things" have slowed down yet. I'm not judging my friend; certainly church attendance is not required for salvation. But I'm afraid that many people postpone their commitment to Jesus with the idea that they will eventually learn about Him and be saved. Our days are limited, and it is a dangerous game to ignore His call and live on our own without Christ in our lives. If you are waiting for an opportunity to give your life to Christ, when "things slow down," I encourage you to stop waiting. You can do it right now, just pray and ask Him to come into your heart. You can use this simple prayer:

> Dear God in heaven, I come to you in the name of Jesus. I acknowledge to You that I am a sinner, and I am sorry for my sins and the life that I have lived; I need your forgiveness.
>
> I believe that your only begotten Son Jesus Christ shed His precious blood on the cross at Calvary and died for my sins, and I am now willing to turn from my sin.
>
> You said in the Bible that if we confess the Lord our God and believe in our hearts that God raised Jesus from the dead, we shall be saved.
>
> Right now I confess Jesus as my Lord. With my heart, I believe that God raised Jesus from the dead. This very moment I accept Jesus Christ

as my own personal Savior, and according to His Word, right now I am saved. Amen.

If you prayed that prayer, your life will change. Typically, it's not an overnight transformation; it's a gradual refinement. Stay connected to Him through prayer and by reading His Word, and you will begin your journey with the Holy Spirit as your guide.

There are various positions relating to when the rapture will take place in relation to something referred to as the seven-year tribulation period. Many believe that Christ was speaking about the tribulation in *Matthew 24:21*, when He said, "*For then there will be great distress, unequaled from the beginning of the world until now—and never to be equaled again.*"

The tribulation is the seven-year period when the wrath of God is poured out on the earth just before the second coming of Jesus. The people of the earth will experience a time of unprecedented suffering. It will be a time of great deception and devastation. Disease will flourish and natural disasters will destroy much of mankind.

Three common explanations with differing viewpoints about when rapture will take place are as follows:

1. Pre-Tribulation: One of the most commonly accepted views holds that the church (believers) will not be required to endure the tribulation. Therefore, Jesus will return prior to the tribulation to take (rapture) His church (His believers), first the dead and then the living, to heaven.
2. Mid-Tribulation: This view teaches that the church will experience the first three and a half years of the tribulation but will be raptured before the final three and a half years.
3. Post-Tribulation: The church will experience the entire seven years of tribulation ending when Jesus comes for all believers and, after the collection of the church is complete, returns and then establishes His kingdom on earth.

If God wanted us to know specifically when Jesus will come back for his church, it would have been spelled out in the Bible. Arguing about our personal interpretations of how or when the rapture will take place doesn't help us at all. However, joining together with other Christians to lovingly discuss and study the return of Christ is inspiring and prepares us for witness to those needing the gospel.

To me the pre-tribulation scenario makes the most sense. I believe that Christ will spare His church the agony brought about by tribulation. Some believe that the reason there are no references to Jesus's church throughout chapters 4 to 18 in Revelation is that the church is no longer on earth because it was "caught up" before tribulation at rapture.

As I mentioned earlier, in *Luke 17:26–27,* Jesus compares His return to the days of Noah, when Noah and his family were spared the wrath of God. *"People were eating, drinking, marrying and being given in marriage up to the day Noah entered the ark. Then the flood came and destroyed them all."* A little further down in *Luke,* in *17:28–29,* Christ also compares the story of Lot, who was spared the fire and sulfur that rained down on Sodom and destroyed the city and all living there. *"It was the same in the days of Lot. People were eating and drinking, buying and selling, planting and building. But the day Lot left Sodom, fire and sulfur rained down from heaven and destroyed them all."*

In both instances, the righteous (Noah, Lot, and their families) were spared God's wrath. It is also interesting to note that in the above scriptures people are eating and drinking, marrying, buying and selling. These activities don't sound like communities that are suffering the tribulation. Interestingly enough, it sounds like our world today.

In *1 Thessalonians 1:9–10* Paul talks about how Jesus will rescue us from the coming wrath, *"They tell how you turned to God from idols to serve the living and true God, and to wait for his Son from heaven, whom he raised from the dead—Jesus, who rescues us from the coming wrath,"* and later in *1 Thessalonians 5:9,* he reminds us that *"God did not appoint us to suffer wrath but to receive salvation through our Lord Jesus Christ."* Perhaps these scriptures are hinting that Christ's church will be spared the terrifying events that will take place during the seven years of tribulation.

Again, there are many theories about when and how and even if the rapture will take place. Let us not let our inconsequential opinions blur the point, and that is, that Christ is coming back for us.

Should a pre-tribulation rapture be accurate, the ramifications are in fact unimaginable for us today. Try and picture what those left behind will experience. Conservative estimates are that there are well over two billion Christians on earth. If the pre-tribulation scenario is accurate, what will be the effect of two billion righteous humans instantly being removed from earth? Imagine the absence of all churches, Christian schools, Christian missions and charities. Envision all Christian doctors, mechanics, lawyers, pilots, politicians, judges, teachers, pastors, and every other righteously consequential individual being removed from the picture in the twinkling of an eye. What will be left? What will be the effect on earth and its remaining inhabitants?

The left-behind population will undoubtedly be severely traumatized when they realize the disappearance of so many. Grief and fear will reign as leaders attempt to explain the phenomenon. We can be sure that Satan will provide misleading explanations to lead the traumatized world away from the fulfillment of Scripture. He will undoubtedly use the widespread confusion and uncertainty to empower his demonic regime.

The stage will be set for the rise of the antichrist and his administration. In *2 Thessalonians 2:7* Paul mentions that the one who holds evil back will be taken out of the way, *"For the secret power of lawlessness is already at work; but the one who now holds it back will continue to do so till he is taken out of the way."* Perhaps Paul is indicating that after rapture, the Holy Spirit will no longer restrain Satan and his evil forces, and thus a profound immorality will be loosed on earth. A new level of wickedness never before seen will begin, and those left behind will be forced to endure until Christ's return.

We must view the return of Christ at rapture with great expectation. He is our Savior and will come to do just that, save us. He will return in glorious fashion to rescue us from this world of sin. We will experience love as never before and be reunited with loved ones. Ours will be a future of splendor, majesty, and adventure.

Later today, or maybe tomorrow, Jesus will come to collect His church. We are told that it will be at an hour that we do not expect Him. So how do we prepare?

God's children stay ready for the return of Jesus by practicing their faith. For most, continually meeting with other Christians to study God's Word is key to maintaining a healthy and vibrant relationship with Jesus. However, many manage to stay close to Jesus while alone, through prayer and study. There is not a set model for maintaining a relationship with Him. He knows our hearts. Jesus assures us, *"I am the good shepherd; I know my sheep and my sheep know me—just as the Father knows me and I know the Father—and I lay down my life for the sheep" (John 10:14–15).*

Perhaps a summary from the American evangelist D. L. Moody will help as we conclude our examination of rapture:

> Before He establishes His kingdom on earth, Jesus will come for His Church, an event commonly referred to as the "Rapture." At that time the dead in Christ will be raised and living Christians will be caught up to meet the Lord in the air and be with Him forever. In this resurrection, those who have died in Christ will have their redeemed souls and spirits united with a body similar to Christ's glorified body. Christians living at the time of this event will not die, but will be changed to be like Christ. This expectation is a motivation for holy living, as well as a source of comfort. No man knows the day or the hour when this will take place.[23]

Christ knows who we are, and He will bring His reward with Him upon His return. Our mission should be to tell others of His wonder and about salvation while we wait. He is the Alpha and the Omega; He is our hope and our Savior. Let's stand tall for Him as we await His return.

---

[23] https://www.moodybible.org/beliefs/positional-statements/second-coming/

CHAPTER 8

The Glorious Return of Jesus

I looked, and there before me was a white cloud, and seated on the cloud was one like a son of man with a crown of gold on his head and a sharp sickle in his hand. Then another angel came out of the temple and called in a loud voice to him who was sitting on the cloud, "Take your sickle and reap, because the time to reap has come, for the harvest of the earth is ripe." So he who was seated on the cloud swung his sickle over the earth, and the earth was harvested.
—Revelation 14:14–16

The book of Acts gives us an astonishing account of the ascension of Jesus. A risen Jesus had just given His disciples the following instructions: *"He said to them: 'It is not for you to know the times or dates the Father has set by his own authority. But you will receive power when the Holy Spirit comes on you; and you will be my witnesses in Jerusalem, and in all Judea and Samaria, and to the ends of the earth"(Acts 1:7–8).*

Amazingly, as He finished with these instructions *"he was taken up before their very eyes, and a cloud hid him from their sight" (verse 9).* As the open-mouthed disciples watched, two men dressed in white stood beside them and said, *"Why do you stand here looking into the sky? This same Jesus, who has been taken from you into heaven will come back in the same way you have seen him go into heaven" (verse 11).*

The angels confirm for us in this passage what Jesus had told the disciples several times: He will return to earth. Until then He is at the right hand of God and is our advocate and intercessor. *"Therefore he is able to save completely those who come to God through him, because he always lives to intercede for them" (Hebrews 7:25).*

Jesus is not coming this time as a humble child in a manger; He is coming to make things right. He is coming to decisively deal with the evil that haunts us in every part of the world today. Jesus will deal with child abuse, human trafficking, genocide, greed, beheadings, mass murders, and every other atrocity we can list. And this time, we will see the Lion of Judah in action as He leads His heavenly army against Satan and his dark forces.

In the pre-tribulation scenario, the Bible tells us that after Christ comes for His church (rapture), the seven-year tribulation period will begin. My focus in this book is not to dive into the details of tribulation or into the prophetic intricacies' foretelling the world events surrounding His return. My prayer is that through these writings we can bring into focus the impending return of our Savior and the wonder that will surely come with Him.

Just before Christ returns to earth, some pretty spectacular and intriguing events take place in heaven. Over five hundred years before Christ, the prophet Daniel records a vision given to him by God describing a heavenly ceremony that will take place. Try and picture what the Bible describes in mysterious detail about what is sometimes referred to as the coronation of Christ. *"I saw in the night visions, and, behold, one like the Son of man came with the clouds of heaven, and came to the Ancient of days, and they brought him near before him. And there was given him dominion, and glory, and a king-*

dom, that all people, nations, and languages, should serve him: his dominion is an everlasting dominion, which shall not pass away, and his kingdom that which shall not be destroyed" (Daniel 7:13–14).

The ceremony described in Daniel will surely be one of the most spectacular events witnessed by any of God's creation. Surely all of heaven will be in awe as its residents observe the holy events.

It is interesting to note that in this scripture, God, referred to as the Ancient of Days, is overseeing the event and presenting Christ with *dominion, glory, and a kingdom.* The previous verses describe God and mention the number of attendees. *"His clothing was as white as snow; the hair of his head was white like wool. His throne was flaming with fire, and its wheels were all ablaze. A river of fire was flowing, coming out from before him. Thousands upon thousands attended him; ten thousand times ten thousand stood before him" (Daniel 7:9–10).* To me, this is undoubtedly the most graphic depiction of God found in the Bible. The scene offers us a glimpse of the structure of the heavenly realm and its proceedings.

In the book of Revelation, Christ revealed to the apostle John the many things that will take place before and after His return. John, along with other criminals, had been exiled to Patmos, a desert island in the Aegean Sea, for crimes they had committed. John was an old man, and the only crime he had committed was to share the news of Jesus with all he met. For this, Domitian, the emperor of Rome, had sent him to Patmos to die.

However, God wasn't yet finished with John. As God so often does, He used this opportunity to provide John with a glimpse of arguably the most amazing sequence of prophetic events to have ever been recorded. John explained that *"On the Lord's Day I was in the Spirit, and I heard behind me a loud voice like a trumpet, which said: 'Write on a scroll what you see and send it to the seven churches: to Ephesus, Smyrna, Pergamum, Thyatira, Sardis, Philadelphia and Laodicea'" (Revelation 1:10–11).*

As instructed, John recorded what was revealed to him in what became the book of Revelation, written around sixty years after the death and resurrection of Jesus. The events that will take place during the tribulation, which precedes His return, are like something out of a science-fiction novel. A leader will emerge who is from Satan and will be as a counterfeit Christ. Many refer to him today using the term *antichrist*. He will establish his kingdom and, along with the *beast* and the *false prophet*, will take control of much of the world, promising great healing and prosperity. The antichrist will try to deceive us by mimicking the work of the Holy Spirit. During the tribulation, Satan will be working to deceive many so that they will turn away from God and turn to his false kingdom.

It will soon become evident that his promises are madness, and major sections of the world will rebel against his administration. This will set the stage for the great world war, referred to in Revelation 16:26 as Armageddon.

The book of Revelation provides in great detail God's agenda throughout these terrible times. But just when things are at their worst, Christ returns to the earth with His heavenly army. "*I saw heaven standing open and there before me was a white horse, whose rider is called Faithful and True. With justice he judges and wages war. His eyes are like blazing fire, and on his head are many crowns. He has a name written on him that no one knows but he himself*" *(Revelation 19:11–12)*.

The Bible tells us that Jesus will first set foot on the Mount of Olives east of Jerusalem. This was the place, interestingly enough, from where He had returned to heaven after His resurrection. This was a significant place for Jesus during His time on earth. "*Each day Jesus was teaching at the temple, and each evening he went out to spend the night on the hill called the Mount of Olives*" *(Luke 21:37)*. Jesus often travelled over the Mount of Olives on His walk from the temple to Bethany. It was from there that He started His triumphal entry to Jerusalem on Palm Sunday. The garden of Gethsemane, which sits at the base of the Mount of Olives, is where He went to pray with His disciples before His arrest. Many other events of significance took place on the Mount of Olives before and during Jesus's time on earth.

We are told that Christ will stand on the Mount of Olives and that the Mount will be "*split in two, from east to west, forming a great valley, with half of the mountain moving north and half moving south*" *(Zechariah 14:4)*.

This day, as described in Zechariah 14:6–7, is a day known only to the Lord. It will be a *unique* day. *"There will be neither sunlight nor cold, frosty darkness."* It will be a day *"with no distinction between day and night,"* but when evening comes, *"there will be light."*

According to GotQuestions.org,[24] one out of every twenty-five verses in the New Testament mentions the Messiah's return. This confirms the profound importance of this momentous day and reveals to us that we must prepare and consider the things that God has planned for us. In the Old Testament, we are told by Amos (3:7) that *"Surely the Sovereign Lord does nothing without revealing his plan to His servants the prophets."* God has offered us ample warning; it is a forewarning we must not overlook, because when Christ returns, He will be ready for war and for judgment. Jesus cautions us to listen to these warnings, *"Whoever has ears to hear, let them hear"* (Mark 4:9).

John goes on to describe what he saw.

> *I saw heaven standing open and there before me was a white horse, whose rider is called Faithful and True. With justice he judges and wages war. His eyes are like blazing fire, and on his head are many crowns. He has a name written on him that no one knows but he himself. He is dressed in a robe dipped in blood, and his name is the Word of God. The armies of heaven were following him, riding on white horses and dressed in fine linen, white and clean. Coming out of his mouth is a sharp sword with which to strike down the nations. "He will rule them with an iron scepter." He treads the winepress of the fury of the wrath of God Almighty. On his robe and on his thigh he has this name written: "KING OF KINGS AND LORD OF LORDS."* (Revelation 19:11–16)

---

[24] Gotquestions.org, *Your Questions. Biblical Answers.*

The *beast* and the kings of the earth with their armies will gather to make war against the rider on the horse and His army. Christ and His army will defeat the enemies of God. The beast and the false prophet will be captured and thrown alive into the fiery lake of burning sulfur. The rest of God's enemies will be killed with the sword that came out of the mouth of the rider on the horse.

I find it amusing when people tell me that they find reading the Bible boring. Come on, is this a wild prophecy or what? The tragedy and wonder of it all, however, is that it is true. These events, my friends, are going to transpire as the world watches. Fear will be rampant. Many will try and hide, but there will be no place to find shelter from this day of retribution.

Revelation 20 starts with an angel coming down from heaven with the keys to the abyss. The abyss, throughout the Bible, is pictured as a bottomless hole in the earth used to contain evil spirits. Some believe that the abyss is where the fallen angels, previously cast out of heaven with Satan, were contained as referenced in *2 Peter 2:4*, "*For if God did not spare angels when they sinned, but sent them to hell, putting them in chains of darkness to be held for judgment.*"

The angel is holding a great chain and seizes Satan and throws him into the abyss to be locked and sealed for a thousand years to keep him from deceiving the nations.

After the business of dealing with Satan is complete, Christ will begin to establish His kingdom on earth. According to the Bible, He will first carry out judgment for those that have survived the great tribulation. "*When the Son of Man comes in his glory, and all the angels with him, he will sit on his glorious throne. All the nations will be gathered before him, and he will separate the people one from another as a shepherd separates the sheep from the goats. He will put the sheep on his right and the goats on his left*" (Matthew 25:31–33).

Those that are found guilty during this judgment are cursed and are condemned "*into the eternal fire prepared for the devil and his angels*" (Matthew 25:41).

The eternal fire represents what should be the most terrifying word in our vocabulary—hell. Jesus warns us in *Matthew 10:28*, "*Do not be afraid of those who kill the body but cannot kill the soul. Rather, be afraid of the One who can destroy both soul and body in hell."*

Hell is the place of misery with no hope of release. Jesus tells us that the unsaved *"will be thrown outside, into the darkness, where there will be weeping and gnashing of teeth" (Matthew 8:12).*

Many people today deny the existence of hell and ridicule those of us that take the Bible seriously on the subject. I am confident that Satan loves to encourage this denial.

As Christians we must stand firm on hell's frightening existence and boldly tell others of the warnings offered in the Bible. Randy Alcorn gives us a great analogy in his book *Heaven* that we can use when discussing hell to those that question its existence. "If you were giving some friends directions to Denver and you knew that one road led there but a second road ended at a sharp cliff around a blind corner, would you talk only about the safe road? No. You would tell them about both, especially if you knew that the road to destruction was wider and more traveled. In fact, it would be terribly unloving not to warn them about that other road."[25]

Those that are separated and designated as "goats" at the judgment will find themselves without hope for eternity. What could be more terrifying? When I think about friends and family that don't seem to give Christ any real consideration, I consider their future and the urgency of sharing the story of Jesus becomes even more pressing.

The souls that survive the judgment will remain on earth, with Jesus, and enjoy a thousand years of peace and blessings. This one-thousand-year period is referred to as the millennial kingdom. The Bible makes it clear several times that this period will be for a thousand years.

During the one-thousand-year period Jesus will establish Himself as king in Jerusalem. This will be a time of peace, and Christ Himself will rule from Jerusalem while Satan is bound and thus unable to deceive mankind.

---

[25] Randy Alcorn. 2004. *Heaven*. Tyndale House Publishers, Inc., Carol Stream, Illinois. p. 26.

The Old Testament prophets referenced this period of time and how Jesus will restore mankind: *"He will judge between the nations and will settle disputes for many peoples. They will beat their swords into plowshares and their spears into pruning hooks. Nation will not take up sword against nation, nor will they train for war anymore" (Isaiah 2:4)*. Perhaps Zechariah is referencing the millennial kingdom in Zechariah 2:10–12, *"'Shout and be glad, Daughter Zion. For I am coming, and I will live among you,' declares the Lord. 'Many nations will be joined with the Lord in that day and will become my people. I will live among you and you will know that the Lord Almighty has sent me to you. The Lord will inherit Judah as his portion in the holy land and will again choose Jerusalem.'"*

This period of time is described so profoundly in Isaac Watts's classic hymn based on Psalm 98, "Joy to the World." Many believe this to be a Christmas song sung to celebrate the birth of Christ. It actually appears, however, to be a celebratory song referencing the return of Jesus to rule the earth.

"Joy to the World, the Lord is come!/Let earth receive her King;/Let every heart, prepare Him room,/And Heaven and nature sing,/And Heaven and nature sing,/And Heaven, and Heaven, and nature sing./He rules the world with truth and grace,/And makes the nations prove/The glories of, His righteousness,/And wonders of His love,/And wonders of His love,/And wonders, wonders, of His love."

At the end of the millennial kingdom, we are told in Revelation 20:7 that Satan will be released for a short time. *"When the thousand years are over, Satan will be released from his prison and will go out to deceive the nations in the four corners of the earth."*

Why would God allow Satan to be released and to start trouble again? Some believe that the children on earth born during the one-thousand-year millennium period must face temptation before the final judgment. These children will have never faced temptation because Satan will be in the abyss during their lives. Perhaps many of these children will reject Jesus due to Satan's influence after his release. However, once again, this remains one of the many mysteries surrounding the return of Jesus.

Satan will be allowed to gather an army from the four corners of the earth. In number they are like "sand on the seashore." They will march across the earth and surround God's people in the city that He loves. Nevertheless, God himself will deal with the army before the battle can even begin. *"They marched across the breadth of the earth and surrounded the camp of God's people, the city he loves. But fire came down from heaven and devoured them"(Revelation 20:9).*

And finally, it is at this time that Satan, the evil one, will reach his journey's end. *"And the devil, who deceived them, was thrown into the lake of burning sulfur, where the beast and the false prophet had been thrown. They will be tormented day and night for ever and ever" (Revelation 20:10).*

The final act will then begin, as every lost sinner will be brought before Christ to stand and be judged. *"Then I saw a great white throne and him who was seated on it. The earth and the heavens fled from his presence, and there was no place for them. And I saw the dead, great and small, standing before the throne, and books were opened. Another book was opened, which is the book of life. The dead were judged according to what they had done as recorded in the books" (Revelation 20:11–12).*

We are told in this passage that the earth and heavens will flee from His presence. This presents such a great mystery, so where will this judgment take place?

The passage also makes it clear that the judgment will be made without consideration of a soul's status on earth. Souls great and small will be treated the same.

We don't know what books are opened with the exception of the Book of Life, which Christ referenced in Revelation 3:5 when talking about the church in Sardis, *"The one who is victorious will, like them, be dressed in white. I will never blot out the name of that person from the book of life, but will acknowledge that name before my Father and his angels."* This book is the transcript of the redeemed, those free from blame, those that will live with Christ forever.

I believe that it is at this point in time that all will perceive the significance of the astonishing gift of grace provided by Jesus. The fallen will then be judged *according to what they had done as recorded in the books.* There will be no chance to defend themselves, and there will be no mercy offered. There will be no grace.

And the judgment will be completed. *"Anyone whose name was not found written in the book of life was thrown into the lake of fire" (Revelation 20:15)*

I appeal to you, the reader, to take a minute and think of the people in your family, or of friends, of your work peers, and yes, even your enemies, those which may not, as far as you know, have their names listed in the Book of Life. Won't you please tell them this story? Won't you take the time and in sincerity, reach out to them, without being prideful, without judgment, and in a non-condescending attitude, tell them about Christ and the wonder of His grace?

It is hard to imagine a world without temptation, illness, disappointment and depression, poverty, sexual immorality, persecution, addiction, and all of the other afflictions put upon mankind in a broken world led by Satan. These things will end, and Christ will be with us on earth.

> *Then I saw a new heaven and a new earth, for the first heaven and the first earth had passed away, and there was no longer any sea. I saw the Holy City, the new Jerusalem, coming down out of heaven from God, prepared as a bride beautifully dressed for her husband. And I heard a loud voice from the throne saying, "Look! God's dwelling place is now among the people, and he will dwell with them. They will be his people, and God himself will be with them and be their God. He will wipe every tear from their eyes. There will be no more death or mourning or crying or pain, for the old order of things has passed away." (Revelation 21:1–4)*

This New Jerusalem is God's kingdom on earth. It will be heaven on earth, and Christ will rule. Christ tells us that He is making *"everything new."* Peter speaks of the New Jerusalem in 2 Peter 3:12–13, *"That day will bring about the destruction of the heavens by fire, and the elements will melt in the heat. But in keeping with his promise we are looking forward to a new heaven and a new earth, where righteousness dwells."*

This will be a place of remarkable blessings. Without Satan to tempt us, and without the curse of the old earth, it will be beyond what our present-day earthly minds can visualize. The apostle John attempted to describe what he saw as an angel carried him away in the Spirit to show him the Holy City, Jerusalem. *"It shone with the glory of God, and its brilliance was like that of a very precious jewel, like a jasper, clear as crystal. It had a great, high wall with twelve gates, and with twelve angels at the gates. On the gates were written the names of the twelve tribes of Israel. There were three gates on the east, three on the north, three on the south and three on the west. The wall of the city had twelve foundations, and on them were the names of the twelve apostles of the Lamb" (Revelation 21:11–14).*

The city's residents will include angels and God's redeemed children. We are told by John that *"The nations will walk by its light, and the kings of the earth will bring their splendor into it. On no day will its gates ever be shut, for there will be no night there. The glory and honor of the nations will be brought into it. Nothing impure will ever enter it, nor will anyone who does what is shameful or deceitful, but only those whose names are written in the Lamb's book of life."*

Thus, all that we know of mankind will come to an end. Those redeemed by Christ will begin a new existence, and we will see the face of Jesus. We are told that we will then reign forever and ever. We will have new heavenly bodies. *"When the perishable has been clothed with the imperishable, and the mortal with immortality" (1 Corinthians 15:54).* Paul confirms this in *Philippians 3:20–21, "But our citizenship is in heaven, and from it we await a Savior, the Lord Jesus Christ, who will transform our lowly body to be like his glorious body, by the power that enables him even to subject all things to himself."*

The Bible offers us enough information on the return of Jesus to challenge and motivate us to seek understanding for the remainder of our lives. It is a story that deserves our sincere and hope-filled consideration. When we immerse ourselves in God's Word and seek answers to our questions, we receive a superabundance of blessings.

For example, the apostle John tells us that we are blessed when we just read or hear the book of Revelation. *"Blessed is the one who reads aloud the words of this prophecy, and blessed are those who hear it and take to heart what is written in it, because the time is near" (Revelation 1:3).*

Friends, lets consistently read and consider the wonderful story presented to us in such an astonishing fashion about the return of Jesus. Our efforts will make us new and enable us to tell His story to those seeking understanding. As John warns us, *"Because the time is near."*

CHAPTER 9

Finish Strong

The night is nearly over; the day is almost here.
—Romans 13:12

A man named Saul from a place called Tarsus, a city in Turkey, remarkably became one of most recognized and faithful followers of Jesus Christ. Saul spoke Greek and was a Jew and was also a member of the religious party called the Pharisees. It is estimated that he was born in 4 BCE, which was about the same time as the birth of Christ.

Saul spent much of his early life persecuting the Christian movement, which he admits to several times in his writings. It is likely that as a Pharisee he traveled from synagogue to synagogue punishing Jews that accepted Christ as the Messiah. We are told in *Acts 8:3, "But Saul began to destroy the church. Going from house to house, he dragged off both men and women and put them in prison."* Saul was good at his trade as evidenced in *Acts 9:1–2, "Meanwhile, Saul was still breathing out murderous threats against the Lord's disciples. He went to the high priest and asked him for letters to the synagogues in Damascus, so that if he found any there who belonged to the Way, whether men or women, he might take them as prisoners to Jerusalem."*

Saul was feared by many and was devoted to crushing the Christian movement until he encountered the risen Jesus.

Saul's conversion is an amazing and mysterious story that changed a fierce persecutor of the early Christian church to a man that suffered greatly throughout his remaining years in support of Jesus. Saul's powerful faith remains an inspiration to anyone studying the New Testament and provides an example of how God can use the most unlikely among us for His purposes.

We are told that Christ confronted Saul on a road to Damascus. *"As he neared Damascus on his journey, suddenly a light from heaven flashed around him. He fell to the ground and heard a voice say to him, 'Saul, Saul, why do you persecute me?' 'Who are you, Lord?' Saul asked. 'I am Jesus, whom you are persecuting,' he replied. 'Now get up and go into the city, and you will be told what you must do.' The men traveling with Saul stood there speechless; they heard the sound but did not see anyone. Saul got up from the ground, but when he opened his eyes he could see nothing. So they led him by the hand into Damascus. For three days he was blind, and did not eat or drink anything"* (Acts 9:3–9).

At this moment Saul was changed. What did Saul experience during and in the days following his Damascus experience? We can be sure that whatever Saul encountered provided a compelling message, for it changed his life forever. At some point, Saul began to use his Roman name, Paul, which means "little" or "small" reflecting a new humility that he found as he became devoted to Christ.

Paul describes in the third person a vision he later had in *1 Corinthians 12:2–4, "I know a man in Christ who fourteen years ago was caught up to the third heaven."* He goes on to explain very briefly his experience in verse 4 when he admits he wasn't sure if he was in his body or apart from his body. He indicates he *"was caught up to paradise and heard inexpressible things, things that no one is permitted to tell."*

What Paul experienced on the Damascus road and in his vision of the third heaven changed him into an apostle that finished strong, really strong. Paul tells us he saw "inexpressible things," and he provided evidence of what he saw later when he spoke about things like the rapture of the church—the return of Jesus with His saints, that we will receive new bodies—and many other things that will take place during the end times.

Of the twenty-seven books in the New Testament, thirteen are accredited to Paul. Paul's unwavering faith continues to encourage us today. Over 2,000 years after his death, his writings continue to change the world by offering us profound insight into what the grace and mercy offered by Jesus can accomplish. Paul offers an example using his own conversion in *1 Timothy 1:15–16, "Christ Jesus came into the world to save sinners—of whom I am the worst. But for that very reason I was shown mercy so that in me, the worst of sinners, Christ Jesus might display his immense patience as an example for those who would believe in him and receive eternal life."*

Paul suffered vicious physical torture, persecution, and eventually martyrdom. He did this that we may hear and receive the wonderful news of Jesus. Friend, we can be like Paul. We can carry forth the message of Jesus in a world just as dark as the one Paul experienced. Paul's voice is echoing loudly across the centuries to us today, *"You then, my son, be strong in the grace that is in Christ Jesus. And the things you have heard me say in the presence of many witnesses entrust to reliable people who will also be qualified to teach others" (2 Timothy 2:1–2).*

Often when I think of Paul my heart aches for a man that gave everything for Christ. Yet he remained humble. I pray that someday I will meet him face-to-face and that we together can continue to thank Jesus for His amazing grace.

Paul's life is a great testimony to the fact that a person's past is not important to Jesus and that Christ often chooses the most unlikely of us to carry out His plans. Christ knows our hearts. Paul affirms that anything is possible with faith in *Philippians 4:13, "I can do all this through him who gives me strength."*

As we contemplate the return of Christ, let us make sure to offer ourselves to His service. Let's strive, as Paul did, forgetting what is behind and straining toward what is ahead, to press on toward the goal to win the prize for which God has called us heavenward in Christ Jesus *(Philippians 3:13–14).*

Have you ever found yourself focusing so much on the small details that you are missing the larger picture? Maybe you've found yourself *not seeing the forest for the trees?* Many of us are guilty of this mistake because we focus so much on the demands of the world that we overlook the grand plan that God has for us. Some of us spend so much time planning our futures we sometimes ignore the largest event that anyone of us will ever face, the return of Jesus.

You say, yes, Kenny, but planning our 401K, choosing the right college for our children, health insurance, career advancement, family vacations, staying fit, new roofs, cars, and yes, even maintaining our yard, are important. And they are. But how do we compare these temporal things to the most astonishing event to ever face mankind? How do we begin to approach something of such consequence that we can't begin to imagine the outcome?

I know, we can't all become contemplative monks and live in a monastery on top of a mountain. So how do we even begin to try to establish the correct perspective?

It starts with offering ourselves to Jesus. To many this may seem like a cliché, but there is nothing in life more important than to be saved. The Philippian jailer who was with Paul and Silas in the prison asked them, *"'Sirs, what must I do to be saved?' They replied, 'Believe in the Lord Jesus, and you will be saved—you and your household'"* (Acts 16:30–31).

Paul tells us in *Romans 10:9, "If you declare with your mouth, 'Jesus is Lord,' and believe in your heart that God raised him from the dead, you will be saved."* And just to be sure, this should be done publicly. Whether you declare your belief to your spouse or in front of your church congregation, profess your faith. Jesus confirmed this when He said, *"Whoever acknowledges me before others, I will also acknowledge before my Father in heaven. But whoever disowns me before others, I will disown before my Father in heaven" (Matthew 10:32–33).*

Most Christians will tell you that after they made the decision to follow Jesus they began to naturally repent of their sins. It's not necessarily a concerted effort, it becomes our desire to turn from what we know is not pleasing to God. Don't get me wrong; there are times we must make a conscious and difficult decision to turn from something we know is sinful. But my point is that if we stay close to Jesus, through the Holy Spirit He will make us aware of the right path and give us the strength we need to follow.

The Holy Spirit invites you, from this moment, to focus more intently on your relationship with Christ. Let's devote the rest of our lives, from this moment that you read these words, until the Lord calls you home, to Christ. Let us *"throw off everything that hinders and the sin that so easily entangles. And let us run with perseverance the race marked out for us" (Hebrews 12:1).*

If we stay in God's Word and study the Scriptures with fellow Christians, surely the Holy Spirit will keep these promises made to us in the Bible:

- *"But seek first the kingdom of God and his righteousness, and all these things will be added to you." (Matthew 6:33)*
- *"But as many as received him, to them gave the power to become the sons of God, even to them that believe on his name." (John 1:12)*
- *"And we know that for those who love God all things work together for good, for those who are called according to his purpose." (Romans 8:28)*
- *"I can do all things through Christ who strengthens me." (Philippians 4:13)*
- *"Let us then with confidence draw near to the throne of grace, that we may receive mercy and find grace to help in time of need." (Hebrews 4:16)*
- *"The one who conquers will be clothed thus in white garments, and I will never blot his name out of the book of life. I will confess his name before my Father and before his angels." (Revelation 3:5)*

These are but a few of the promises that God will deliver if we will just make an effort to follow Jesus. Test Him, and you will see that His Word is true and that He is faithful to us.

You may be reading this and think that it's a little late in life for you to change and to finish strong. Nonsense, it is never too late for

God to appoint you to make a difference. Confess your shortcomings to the Lord and ask Him to come into your heart and you will be amazed at what will happen. The truly exciting thing is that His plan for you will probably be a surprise; nevertheless, it will be exactly what you are meant to do. Trust Him.

When I think of a wonderful example of finishing strong, I think about the story of David and Svea Flood. David was a Swede who gave his life to Christ at a young age. He married Svea, and they felt called to serve Jesus in Africa and thus traveled there in 1921. They wanted to work among people who had never heard the gospel. Their service was difficult, and the people were hostile and not receptive. The conditions were horrible, and the work was hard. Additionally, their lives were constantly in danger.

The Floods were raising two children in those conditions, and shortly after the second child was born, Svea died. David, already having doubts about the ministry and discouraged by the lack of results, was overwhelmed. Their efforts had produced just one convert, a young boy. He had sacrificed his wife and the best years of his life. For what, for one convert?

David felt that he had been a fool for bringing Svea to that inhospitable place and was overcome with grief and guilt. He decided to leave Africa defeated. He took his young son with him, but tragically he had to leave his infant daughter behind since she was too ill to travel.

A missionary couple took her in, and she was passed to a second couple after the first missionaries passed away. The second missionary couple took her to America where they raised her. David, who was living in Sweden, lost his faith. He married and divorced and began to live with a mistress. He thought little of the daughter whom he had not seen since she was a baby.

His daughter, Aggie, however, thought about him often. She had been told about the work he and her mother had begun in Africa, and this made her want to talk with her father. As she grew older, Aggie married and lived in America with her husband. However, she continued to want to meet and talk with her father.

Years later she arranged a trip to Sweden and found her seventy-three-year-old father, bedridden and living in a shabby apartment littered with liquor bottles. She told her father that she loved him and that God also loved him and wanted him to come back to his faith. And then she told him about his one convert.

That little boy had grown up to be a gifted leader and minister of the gospel. That one little boy eventually led thousands of others to Christ and helped to establish the church of Jesus Christ in that section of Africa. Upon hearing what God had done, David threw himself on the mercy of God. He asked God to forgive his rebellion and wasted years. And God did. David didn't know that he had just six months to live. But those six months were months of productivity and enabled David to restore broken relationships.

After nearly forty years of falling on his face, David Flood got up and finished the race. And David, after his long journey, came back to his faith and finished strong.[26]

We are not all meant to serve on a mission in Africa. But we must seek to serve Him in our own way. The Holy Spirit will assist us in our search. And like David Flood, we may not see the fruit of our efforts until later. We may not recognize any good achievement while we are on earth. But we must be content in knowing that our Lord can do miraculous things with our humble undertakings and that none of our efforts are wasted.

We have a limited number of days left on earth; therefore, it is important that we consistently seek a closer relationship with Christ. At the same time, we must reach out to others to share the gospel and to demonstrate its effect on our lives. Consistent study of God's Word, prayer, and fellowship with other Christians will prepare us to be of service. May the Holy Spirit lead you as you finish strong.

[26] Ruth Tucker. *Stories of Faith* (Grand Rapids, Zondervan,1989), as told in Steve Farrar's *Finishing Strong* (Multnomah Publishers, Inc., 1995).

CHAPTER 10

The Beauty That Awaits Us

The man who is about to sail for Australia or New Zealand as a settler is naturally anxious to know something about his future home, its climate, its employments, its inhabitants, its ways, its customs. All these are subjects of deep interest to him. You are leaving the land of your nativity, you are going to spend the rest of your life in a new hemisphere. It would be strange indeed if you did not desire information about your new abode. Now surely, if we hope to dwell forever in that "better country, even a heavenly one," we ought to...try to become acquainted with it.

—J C Ryle

In his book *Where I Am*, the late Billy Graham tells a story about a mother and son that once lived in a miserable attic. Years before, she had married against her parents' wishes and had gone with her husband to live in a strange land. But her husband soon died, and she managed with great difficulty to secure the bare necessities. The boy's happiest times were when his mother told of her father's house in the old country, a place with grassy lawns, enormous trees, wide porches, and delicious meals. The child longed to live there.

One day the postman knocked at the door with a letter. The woman recognized her father's handwriting and, with trembling fingers, opened the envelope that held a check and a slip of paper with two words: "Come home."[27]

One day, as Christians, we will be called home. It is surprising to me that we seldom speak with each other about our heavenly home. I mean, if we truly believe that it is our eternal place of residence, shouldn't we at least talk with each other from time to time about our final destination? Our imaginations wander as we consider the possibility of alien life on other planets, the existence of ghosts, and many other paltry subjects. Shouldn't we try and imagine what a heavenly existence will be like?

If we really think about it, we are just a few heartbeats away from beginning a new life in an eternal realm; literally, you can be transported to heaven before you get up from reading this book. And it's not *if* it happens, it's *when*. In fact, approximately 161,517 people die every day on planet Earth. That's 6,730 per hour, 112 per minute.[28] As with the billions of souls that have moved on, so it will be with us.

Furthermore, death is not something of which we should be afraid. We are presented encouraging glimpses of heaven throughout the Bible. The apostle John explained as best he could, this amazing sight.

> *Then the angel showed me the river of the water of life, as clear as crystal, flowing from the throne of God and of the Lamb down the middle of the great street of the city. On each side of the river stood the tree of life, bearing twelve crops of fruit, yielding*

---

[27] Billy Graham. 2015. *Where I Am*. W Publishing Group, an Imprint of Thomas Nelson.

[28] Worldpopulationreview.com

its fruit every month. And the leaves of the tree are
for the healing of the nations. No longer will there
be any curse. The throne of God and of the Lamb
will be in the city, and his servants will serve him.
They will see his face, and his name will be on their
foreheads. There will be no more night. They will
not need the light of a lamp or the light of the sun,
for the Lord God will give them light. And they will
reign for ever and ever. (Revelation 22:1–5)

This is an astonishing testimony by John and should excite us and we ponder what he describes. For example, what will the *river of the water of life* and *the tree of life* John saw offer to us? Some surmise that the crystal clear river could be a continual outpouring of the Holy Spirit. Some suggest that the tree of life is the same tree that was in the garden in Genesis and will provide a divine sustenance through its twelve crops of fruit yielded every month. These are intriguing topics to consider. And we should consider them, because doing so brings us closer to understanding God's promised kingdom.

So the question remains, why don't we speak of heaven frequently?

In his excellent book *Heaven*, Randy Alcorn points out our lack of focus on heaven. "Many Christians who've gone to church all their adult lives (especially those under fifty) can't recall having heard a single sermon on heaven. It's occasionally mentioned, but rarely emphasized, and almost never is it developed as a topic. We're told how to get to heaven, and that it's a better destination than hell, but we're taught remarkably little about heaven itself." [29]

Perhaps the experience of Dr. Mary Neal provides a glimpse of what awaits God's children in heaven. In 1999 in a region of southern Chile, a board-certified orthopedic spine surgeon, Dr. Mary Neal, drowned in a kayak accident. Dr. Neal was without oxygen for twenty-four minutes and, during her event, experienced life after

---

[29] Randy Alcorn. 2004. *Heaven.* Tyndale House Publishers, Inc., Carol Stream, Illinois. p. 10.

death and went to heaven. She witnessed many wonderful things and was subsequently returned to earth. While in heaven she conversed with Jesus and was given a glimpse of the wonders that await all believers. She was returned to earth with a mission. Her story has inspired millions to live by faith and is a story of great hope for us all.

Dr. Neal suffered two broken legs and an injury to her lungs as a result of the incident and spent a month in the hospital. As a doctor, she is accustomed to having a biological explanation for near-death phenomena like bright lights and warm feelings. However, Dr. Neal is convinced her experience was a different situation.

Dr. Neal described part of her experience in an interview with *Christianity Today* in December 2012.[30]

> Eventually we did get to the big arched entryway, and inside I could see many, many other spirits, angels, people—I don't know what they were. They were all running around. They were all very busy, and I'm not sure what they were doing, but I knew that they were busy doing God's work. When I arrived they looked up and had this same sense of absolute joy at my arrival. Another profound part of the experience—and again, I can't explain it using three-dimensional language: During that time, it became absolutely clear to me that these people were joyful not only at my arrival but at the arrival of every person who shows up. More importantly, I understood how God can actually know each one of us, love each one of us as though we were the only one, and can have an incredible plan for each one of us. That's something that before this experience was difficult for me to grasp. But during this

30 "Mary Neal Describes Her Visit to the Gates of Heaven." Mark Galli Interviews Dr. Mary Neal *Christianity Today*. December 6, 2012

time, it became absolutely clear to me how that can be, and how all of God's promises are true.

Dr. Neal's experience and others like it offer us hope and should encourage us to live focused on our final destination, heaven. If we really believe that we are heading toward a beautiful place designed for us by our Creator, shouldn't the things of this world move down on our priority list and the things we do for Christ's kingdom move up? Shouldn't our focus each day be centered on living in the presence of Christ? The answer to these questions is unquestionably yes.

Charles Spurgeon, the English pastor sometimes referred to as the "Prince of Preachers," offers us great advice and insight as we consider our destination.

> And what know we of the journey? And what know we of the country to which we are bound? A little we have read thereof, and somewhat has been revealed to us by the Spirit; but how little do we know of the realms of the future! We know that there is a black and stormy river called "Death." God bids us cross it, promising to be with us. And, after death, what cometh? What wonder-world will open upon our astonished sight? What scene of glory will be unfolded to our view? No traveler has ever returned to tell. But we know enough of the heavenly land to make us welcome our summons thither with joy and gladness. The journey of death may be dark, but we may go forth on it fearlessly, knowing that God is with us as we walk through the gloomy valley, and therefore we need fear no evil. We shall be departing from all we have known and loved here, but we shall be going to our Father's house-to our Father's home, where Jesus is—to that royal "city which hath foundations, whose builder and maker is God." This shall be our last

removal, to dwell forever with him we love, in the midst of his people, in the presence of God. Christian, meditate much on heaven, it will help thee to press on, and to forget the toil of the way. This vale of tears is but the pathway to the better country: this world of woe is but the stepping-stone to a world of bliss.[31]

I like to think about the wonder-world Spurgeon references. I picture in my mind the garden that God prepared for Adam and Eve. *"Now the Lord God had planted a garden in the east, in Eden; and there he put the man he had formed. The Lord God made all kinds of trees grow out of the ground—trees that were pleasing to the eye and good for food. In the middle of the garden were the tree of life and the tree of the knowledge of good and evil"* (Genesis 2:8–9). God Himself prepared the garden specifically for them. Matthew Henry describes his view of the garden as follows:

> The place appointed for Adam's residence was a garden; not an ivory house nor a palace overlaid with gold, but a garden, furnished and adorned by nature, not by art. What little reason have men to be proud of stately and magnificent buildings, when it was the happiness of man in innocence that he needed none! As clothes came in with sin, so did houses. The heaven was the roof of Adam's house, and never was any roof so curiously ceiled and painted. The earth was his floor, and never was any floor so richly inlaid. The shadow of the trees was his retirement; under them were his dining rooms, his lodging rooms, and never were any rooms so finely hung as these: Solomon's, in all their glory, were not arrayed like them.[32]

---

[31] Charles Spurgeon. 1997. *Morning and Evening*. Hendrickson Publishers.
[32] Matthew Henry. 1706–1721. *Commentary on the Whole Bible*.

I try and imagine the trees and flowers displaying colors I've never seen. Dr. Mary Neal describes how colors were presented her near-death experience. "When I saw the colors, it's as though I understood them. I saw them, I could taste them, I could hear them. I understood their very essence. And I realize none of this makes sense in our language, but that's what it was."[33]

I imagine the aromas and the sounds that will surround us. I know that we will be overwhelmed with sensations not before experienced.

I can even imagine a small cottage specifically designed for me by the One who knows me better than I know myself. As I explore my new home I envision myself uncovering small gifts or trinkets that will touch my heart and will somehow explain my character and personality to me. And there will be music drifting throughout my new home, music that is in harmony with my soul and brings me peace but at the same time motivates me.

I will no longer be rushed through life. I know I will be content in the moment and thus able to appreciate the wonder that surrounds me. This will enable me to explore my creativity and to use it to serve Jesus.

More than anything, I am convinced that I will be overwhelmed in the fact that I am home. I will be in the home that God intended for us all before the fall of mankind.

Insecurities and worry will no more haunt me. I will be confident in my existence, and I will have a purpose, a purpose designed for me by my Creator. It will be a purpose that fits me perfectly.

I think about people who have experienced severe difficulties in their lives on earth and the fantastic change that awaits them in heaven. People who are blind or have serious physical or mental impairments.

The Christian author Joni Eareckson Tada became a quadriplegic when diving into the Chesapeake Bay after misjudging the shal-

---

[33] "Dr. Mary C. Neal Recalls Her Inspiring Near-Death Experience." *Guideposts Magazine.* Video Library.

lowness of the water in 1967. In her book *Heaven: Your Real Home,* she describes what she believes awaits her when she reaches heaven.

> I still can hardly believe it. I, with shriveled, bent fingers, atrophied muscles, gnarled knees, and no feeling from the shoulders down, will one day have a new body, light, bright, and clothed in righteousness—powerful and dazzling. Can you imagine the hope this gives someone spinal cord-injured like me? Or someone who is cerebral palsied, brain-injured, or who has multiple sclerosis? Imagine the hope this gives someone who is manic-depressive. No other religion, no other philosophy promises new bodies, hearts, and minds. Only in the gospel of Christ do hurting people find such incredible hope.[34]

I enthusiastically anticipate receiving the tidal wave of love that will surely flow over each of us when we are received by Christ and the saints. Peter writes about a *"rich welcome into the eternal kingdom of our Lord and Savior" (2 Peter 1:11).* Encountering Christ will be a moment long awaited by so many. I can only imagine the exhilaration that will fill my soul as never before. Surely angels and loved ones will surround us, and God's promises will be fulfilled as never imagined.

Trudy Harris, RN, is the former president of the Hospice Foundation for Caring. She was a hospice nurse for many years before moving on to become president. In her book *Glimpses of Heaven: True Stories of Hope and Peace at the End of Life's Journey,* Mrs. Harris offers us touching stories of forty-four people and their last moments on earth. I find her insight compelling and her experiences reassuring.

---

[34] Joni Eareckson Tada. 1995. *Heaven: Your Real Home.* Grand Rapids: Zondervan. p. 53.

In the introduction of her book, she describes those for which she provided care as entering into a pure orientation as they were preparing to die.

> This temporary tent, which is our body, is changing, and no one knows this better than the person who is dying. If you sit quietly and listen to them, both their questions and their insights, they will invite you to share in this next, awesome step in life's journey. There is nothing left to hide, nothing to gain, and nothing to prove or lose, thus making the sharing totally pure. And when you enter into the wonderment of these blessed experiences with them. You yourself will grow.[35]

As I previously mentioned, many people see angels or family members as death draws closer. Mrs. Harris goes on to describe these visions that some experience.

> When they spoke of angels, which many did, the angels were always described as more beautiful than they had ever imagined, eight feet tall, male, and wearing a white for which there is no word. "Luminescent" is what each one said, like nothing they had ever seen before. The music they spoke of was far more exquisite than any symphony they had ever heard, and over and over again they mentioned colors that they said were too beautiful to describe.

---

[35] Trudy Harris, RN. 2008. *Glimpses of Heaven: True Stories of Hope and Peach at the End of Life's Journey.* Fall River Press. p. 18.

In the conclusion of her book, Mrs. Harris provides a summary of what she has surmised over her time serving as a hospice nurse.

> People frequently have asked me, "What is the most important thing you have learned over the last thirty-two years of caring for friends, family members and patients who were terminally ill and dying?" My answer, without hesitation, is now and always has been that God simply loves each and every person He has ever created, warts and all. It is His wish that not one be lost. The extent to which He will go to make this happen is awesome to see and touch and feel. It is palpable in all the experiences God allows His children to have as He is preparing to take them home to Himself.
>
> Dying is a very natural part of living. It is not an ending but a beginning. A transition into the life God has promised to all of His children. He wants us home with Him when we finish the work He created us to do. He loves us—believe it.[36]

Most of the souls created by God will experience death before Jesus returns. Some will be taken from earth and transformed without dying either at rapture or upon Jesus's second coming. Nevertheless, we have a divine appointment scheduled. We will be summoned and will encounter Christ face-to-face. It will happen in just a moment, very quickly, and we will immediately realize, as never before in our lives, that the events promised in the Bible are true.

It is with love and sincere hope that I speak to you, the reader of this book. Presently, in 2020, life has taken some rather abrupt turns, and the pressures of life are taking their toll on many of us. Hold on,

---

[36] Trudy Harris, RN. 2008. *Glimpses of Heaven: True Stories of Hope and Peach at the End of Life's Journey.* Fall River Press. p. 190.

dear Christian. It will be just a minute before our Savior will rescue us from our burdens.

Christ is going to return. And those that have already passed on and those still alive will receive the amazing gift of something called *redemption*. Redemption is the act of buying something back or paying a price or ransom to return something to your possession. Simply put, Jesus, through His sacrificial death, has saved us from the slavery of sin to set us free from bondage. He is our redeemer.

We will be transported to a place so beautiful it will exceed any expectation we have, and sin will be no more. Everyone we meet will be who they were created to be, and we will connect on a level never before experienced.

God offers us a peek at what awaits us through Isaiah, written approximately 2,700 years ago: *"See, I will create new heavens and a new earth. The former things will not be remembered, nor will they come to mind. But be glad and rejoice forever in what I will create, for I will create Jerusalem to be a delight and its people a joy. I will rejoice over Jerusalem and take delight in my people; the sound of weeping and of crying will be heard in it no more"* (Isaiah 65:17–19).

Friends, Jesus is coming back. It is not fantasy, as some would have you believe. So many scoff at Christians when we speak of His return. Many of these same people curse using His name, and if you speak about Jesus with respect, or pray in His name, they claim they are offended and lash out. Don't be discouraged. Unfortunately multitudes of these people will find themselves terrified as they experience the promise described by Jesus Himself in *Matthew 13:40–42*, *"As the weeds are pulled up and burned in the fire, so it will be at the end of the age. The Son of Man will send out his angels, and they will weed out of his kingdom everything that causes sin and all who do evil. They will throw them into the blazing furnace, where there will be weeping and gnashing of teeth."*

Are you ready for the return of Jesus? If you're not sure, just pray and ask Him for help in preparing. He will answer that prayer. And one day in the future, you and I will be together and we will be truly astonished at the wonderful existence we will share. We will begin a magnificent adventure, which, to our amazement, will not grow old but will continue to inspire us. Until then, my friends, I remain yours in the hope that we will share the adventure together.

"Do not let your hearts be troubled. You believe in God; believe also in me. My Father's house has many rooms; if that were not so, would I have told you that I am going there to prepare a place for you? And if I go and prepare a place for you, I will come back and take you to be with me that you also may be where I am" (John 14:1–3).

ABOUT THE AUTHOR

Kenny Underwood grew up in Newport News, Virginia. He and his wife, Nancy, later moved to a small beach community in Virginia Beach where they lived for twenty-eight years and raised their three children: Zachary, Matthew, and Mollie. Kenny spent half of his career with AT&T and later established Underwood Communications, a telecommunications consulting firm in Virginia Beach.

Kenny has been active in his service for Jesus over the years in several ministries, including the YouTube channel One-Minute-Sermon.com, and in his involvement in the Walk to Emmaus movement.

Kenny and his wife, Nancy, live in Wake, Virginia.

CPSIA information can be obtained
at www.ICGtesting.com
Printed in the USA
BVHW031923020322
630505BV00004B/140